The Capability Code
How to Stay Independent, Sharp, and Powerful for Life

Ivette Smith

Table of Contents

Introduction: The Price of Toughness

I'm 58 years old with hardware where my right shoulder used to be.

Not a rod or a few pins—a complete reverse total shoulder replacement. They took out what was left of my rotator cuff, ball joint, and socket, and gave me titanium and polyethylene parts assembled in reverse configuration. The mechanics of my shoulder now work backwards from how human shoulders are supposed to function, forcing previously minor muscles to do the work my destroyed rotator cuff can no longer perform.

This is the kind of surgery usually reserved for elderly patients in their late 70s or 80s with severe degenerative arthritis. I had it at 56.

The surgery forced me to resign from my job in January 2022. I haven't worked outside the home since. I'm in what should be my peak earning years—the decade where experience meets capability, where you mentor others while building retirement security. Instead, I'm permanently disabled because I spent decades doing exactly what I was taught to do: push through the pain, prove I'm not weak, never quit.

This book is 90 percent science-backed information, 10percent me.

Let me tell you how I got here.

The First Injury (Or: When "Just Get It Done" Becomes Permanent)

I was an inspector, and we received a shipment of items in a completely destroyed crate. Three thousand items, each weighing about 25 pounds, scattered and exposed. I had to recrate every single one of them.

I was alone. Uncharacteristically, because our operations required, for the most part, two people.

I couldn't leave the items outside overnight—security protocol, weather exposure, accountability requirements, take your pick of the reasons it "had to be done" immediately. So I pressed on. Hour after hour, lifting, organizing, repacking. Twenty-five pounds isn't much, right? Except when you do it three thousand times in rapid succession, overhead, at awkward angles, with no rest, no help, and no option to stop.

By the time I realized I'd messed something up in my right shoulder, I switched to my left arm. But it was too late. The damage was done.

When I woke up the next morning, I couldn't move my right arm without excruciating pain. In the military, you don't just call in sick. You report to the clinic for assessment first, then call your supervisor with the "suggested plan of action to make me better as quickly as possible." Translation: How fast can we get you back to duty?

I couldn't do physical therapy first because I literally couldn't move the arm. The doctor insisted on imaging. X-rays, then an MRI. His verdict: surgery first, PT after.

That was injury number one.

The Pattern Emerges (Or: When Your Body Becomes Collateral Damage)

I think I averaged a surgery every three years after that. I've honestly lost count of how many there were—seven? Eight? At some point, after years of overcompensating with my left arm because my right was compromised, the left shoulder went out too.

Some injuries had obvious causes. Like the times I helped colleagues load weapons onto trailers during nighttime operations. The weapon systems weighed 188 pounds and required a three-man lift. Except there was no third person, so up we went—over our heads, onto the trailer, just the two of us. How many times can you do that without consequences? I don't know, but it didn't take me long to be broken again.

Some injuries were mysterious. I'd wake up one morning in pain despite having done nothing strenuous lately. Apparently, I have weak tendons—a fact I only learned after years of them repeatedly failing under stress. In these cases, we did PT first, and when that didn't resolve it, I went under the knife again. Six weeks to recover from something I now know takes six months to a year to fully heal.

Then it was back to business as usual, setting myself up for the next injury, the next surgery, the next desperate attempt to prove I wasn't lazy or incompetent.

At least one injury happened while I was having fun. Kayaking with friends in the Dominican Republic—by the time we finished for the night, I was broken again. Didn't realize it until I went to the gym with my trainer a few weeks later, couldn't use certain weight machines without severe pain. Hospital. Imaging. Surprise: broken again.

The Gender Factor (Or: The Extra Cost of Being "Excess Baggage")

Here's what I haven't mentioned yet: I was a woman in a mostly male career field. I was already written off as excess baggage before I even proved myself.

So I lifted heavier. Worked longer. Never complained. Never asked for help—not when I needed it, and certainly not before I absolutely had to. I pushed through injuries that should have sidelined me. I did the 188-pound "three-man" lifts. I recrated those 3,000 items alone. I hurt myself doing push-ups trying to demonstrate I was capable, and when people looked at me skeptically, I pushed even harder.

By 2001, I was tired of overdoing it to prove myself to a few cavemen. Let them underestimate me, I thought. That'll be fun.

It wasn't fun. It was career-ending.

The Discharge (Or: When Your Broken Body Becomes Inconvenient)

In 2008, I was medically discharged. The official reason? Sleep apnea.

Not the destroyed shoulders. Not the cascade of surgeries. Not the chronic pain or limited mobility or the fact that my body was breaking down from decades of impossible demands. Sleep apnea. Right before I left I was given a parting gift. Guess what? You have Multiple Sclerosis. An autoimmune disease that eats the myelin off your nerves. Yipee!

I took my discharge and left the service with multiple chronic problems, and a bitter taste in my mouth, which the Veterans Affairs Department later addressed. But the damage was done. The pattern was set. And it followed me into civilian life.

The Civilian Sequel (Or: Same Story, Different Uniform)

By 2010, I was working as an office manager—which somehow morphed into also being the warehouse person, and eventually, doing everything that needed to be done. After two grueling days preparing a shipment of Dish equipment, my right arm complained and objected strenuously to movement.

Here we go again. Worker's compensation case because the injury happened at work. After three years with that company, I was replaced. The surgery and recovery time were too long. They needed someone whose body still worked. And needed them now.

For once, I was going to have all the time in the world to heal.

I couldn't work until the workers' comp process discharged me, so I was receiving short-term and then long-term disability. With help from the Veterans Affairs office, I managed to go back to school for a BS in Information Technology. That took me through 2016 with no major physical injuries—though I was shopping for work incessantly because I was terrified of running out of income, terrified I would become indigent.

Just when I was resigned that poverty might be my lot in life, my now-last employer called and offered me a job. I accepted and worked for six years, happy as a clam. Almost.

I say "almost" because I had bipolar episodes during that time, and those are usually not good—especially when you're not medicated. Bipolar mania alters pain perception. You don't feel injuries the way you should. You push harder because you literally can't recognize your body's warning signals.

One day in December 2021, I picked up my 20-pound tool bag at the wrong angle.

That was it.

I didn't know it for sure in that moment, but I knew I'd hurt myself. Again.

The Final Surgery (Or: When "Not Salvageable" Becomes Your Reality)

Workers' compensation again. The process: PT before surgery—sure, why not extend my pain while we try the conservative approach that we both know won't work.

Finally, it was concluded that because I'd had so many injuries and surgeries, my shoulder was not salvageable. The rotator cuff was too damaged, the joint too compromised, the surrounding structures too weakened by decades of trauma and surgical intervention.

They had to go for the most serious option: reverse total shoulder replacement surgery.

There was a "come to Jesus" conversation before the procedure. I could live the rest of my life with severely limited arm movement—maybe 45 degrees of range—or I could undergo this procedure where they would reverse the mechanics of my shoulder joint, forcing previously weaker muscles and tendons to learn an entirely new movement range and have almost 80% of range back.

They gave me a new shoulder made of hardware. But it would never be the same. It would never be whole.

In January 2022, I resigned from my position. I was 56 years old.

Since then, I have not held a job outside the home.

The Recovery (Or: Redefining Strength at 58)

I started exercising more carefully. I picked up Pilates. I continued physical therapy at home, learning my new limitations, building what strength I could within them. I was doing okay until another bipolar episode presented itself, reminding me that mental and physical health are inseparable.

I started art journaling. Arts and crafts. Trying to stay busy, trying to maintain identity and purpose when my body had taken so much from me. Meditation. And last but not least, I started writing.

So here I am. Fifty-eight years old. Hardware in my shoulder. Unable to work outside the home. Living with the permanent consequences of decades spent believing that pain was weakness leaving the body, that pushing through was strength, that asking for help was failure. This was a load of manure. But I guess, most of us couldn't smell it at the time.

Why I'm Writing This Book

I can't undo my injuries. I can't get back the career I lost. I can't erase the surgeries, the chronic pain, the years of damage accumulating while I powered through.

But I can tell you the truth.

"No pain, no gain" is a lie.

Pain is information. It's your body communicating that something is wrong, that you need to stop, that continuing will cause damage. Ignoring that information has consequences. And those consequences compound over decades—quietly, invisibly, until one day you wake up and your body simply can't do it anymore.

This book is not just about aging. It's about the specific kind of aging that happens when you spend decades in a culture that normalizes the impossible, punishes vulnerability, and treats your body as a tool to be used until it breaks.

It's about military fitness culture, yes. But it's also about athletics, first responder work, nursing, corporate pressure-cooker environments, and any other high-performance culture where "tough it out" becomes doctrine. It's especially about what happens to women in these environments—how the need to prove we're "not weak" or "not excess baggage" drives us to destroy ourselves faster and more thoroughly than our male counterparts.

This book combines everything I've learned about the biology of aging, the science of injury, the cascade of compensatory damage, and the long road of recovery. It's the research I did too late, the interventions I should have made decades ago, and the hard-won wisdom of someone who learned everything the hardest way possible.

Who This Book Is For

If you've spent years pushing through pain, this book is for you.

If you've been taught that asking for help is weakness, this book is for you.

If you're a woman who spent her career proving she wasn't "excess baggage," this book is for you.

If you're in your 30s or 40s and you're starting to notice that old injuries aren't healing like they used to, this book is for you.

If you're in your 50s or 60s and you're paying the price for decades of "no excuses" mentality, this book is for you.

If you're a veteran, former athlete, first responder, nurse, or anyone from a high-performance culture that taught you to ignore your body's signals—this book is for you.

What You'll Find in These Pages

This book guides you through the science of aging, the reality of cumulative damage, and the path to recovery and sustainable strength.

You'll learn about biological changes after 30, cellular aging, hormonal shifts, and injury cascades. You'll understand nutrition, exercise, mental health, and social connections. You'll discover preventative strategies and recovery techniques.

But more than that, you'll see what all of this looks like in real life—my life. Every scientific explanation is grounded in lived experience. Every piece of advice comes from both research and consequence.

The Timeline of Damage

Throughout this book, you'll see references to my Timeline of Damage—a chart that lays out what I did, what was happening in my body, and what it cost me. It's brutal. But it shows the pattern so you can recognize it in yourself.

If you're in your 30s or 40s, you still have time. If you're in your 50s or 60s, you can still recover and rebuild. But you have to stop believing the lie that pain equals progress.

TIMELINE OF DAMAGE

The Cumulative Cost of "No Pain, No Gain"

AGE / DECADE	EVENT	PHYSICAL COST	FINANCIAL COST
Early 20s 1990s	**First Major Injury: The Crate Incident**	Severe damage to right shoulder requiring surgery; unable to move arm; switched to left arm and damaged that too	Covered by military healthcare
Mid-Late 20s 1990s	**Pattern Emerges: "Salad Week" & Crash Dieting**	Metabolic damage from repeated crash diets before fitness tests; muscle loss; hormonal disruption	Covered by military healthcare
20s-30s 1990s-2000s	**Chronic Dehydration Protocols**	Kidney damage from manipulating water intake for weigh-ins; joint damage (cartilage needs water)	Covered by military healthcare (damage accumulating for future costs)
30s 2000s	**Surgery Every ~3 Years Pattern**	Multiple orthopedic surgeries; chronic pain develops; range of motion decreases with each cycle	Covered by military healthcare

Mid 30s 2000s	**Kayaking Injury in Dominican Republic**	Additional shoulder damage; reinforcement that body can't handle "normal" activities	Emergency care abroad + follow-up covered by military
Late 30s-40s 2000s	**Gender Factor: Overcompensation Injuries**	Lifting heavier, working longer to prove worth; accelerated deterioration	Covered by military healthcare
2008 (Age ~40)	**MEDICAL DISCHARGE FROM AIR FORCE**	Officially for "sleep apnea" - actual reason: cumulative injury making continued service impossible	LOSS OF MILITARY HEALTHCARE - Financial costs begin here
40s 2010s	**Post-Discharge: Cumulative Effects Compound**	Menopause + existing injuries = exponential deterioration; hormone loss accelerates joint damage	OUT-OF-POCKET COSTS BEGIN: Multiple specialists, limited insurance coverage, medication expenses
40s-50s 2010s-2020s	**Escalating Medical Needs**	Ongoing pain management; adaptive equipment; ergonomic modifications; physical therapy (when affordable)	Thousands in annual out-of-pocket costs; insurance denials; treatment gaps due to cost

Age 56 2022	**THE FINAL SURGERY: Reverse Total Shoulder Replacement**	Hardware where shoulder used to be; surgery for patients typically in their 70s-80s; shoulder "not salvageable"	MAJOR SURGICAL COSTS; Forced resignation from IT job (Jan 2022); Loss of income
Age 56-58 2022-2024	**Recovery & New Reality**	Chronic pain; severe mobility limitations; can only work from home; limited physical capacity	Ongoing medical expenses with no employer insurance; accumulating debt from years of costs
Age 58 PRESENT	**Current State: The Bill Comes Due**	Reverse shoulder replacement; chronic pain; multiple declining systems; limited mobility	SECOND MORTGAGE: ~$150,000 to cover accumulated debt; Retirement savings: virtually nothing; Costs ongoing

KEY INSIGHT: Physical damage accumulated while in the military (with healthcare coverage), but financial devastation began AFTER 2008 discharge when forced to cover ongoing costs from decades of cumulative injury out-of-pocket. The injuries were created in the 20s-30s; the financial crisis arrived in the 40s-50s.

A Note on Vulnerability

Writing this required more vulnerability than I've ever shown. I've had to own my shame about being "broken," my anger at a system that normalized my destruction, and my grief over a career cut short.

This vulnerability is intentional. The only way to break the cycle is to be honest about its cost.

The Promise

This book won't give you your body back if it's already broken. It won't undo surgeries or erase chronic pain.

But it will validate your experience, explain what's happening, offer recovery strategies, and show you how to age strong despite your past.

Let's Begin

Welcome to "The Cost of 'No Pain, No Gain.'" This is not a gentle book about aging gracefully. This is an unflinching examination of what happens when we sacrifice our bodies on the altar of toughness—and a practical guide to recovery despite the damage.

I'm 58 with hardware in my shoulder, and I'm still learning what strength really means.

Let me show you what I've learned.

Chapter 1: Laying the Foundations for Longevity

When you wake up on the morning of your 30th birthday, you might not feel any different. I certainly didn't. I was in the Air Force, physically fit by all the standards that mattered—could pass the fitness test, could lift the required weight, could run the required distance. I felt invincible.

What I didn't know was that my body had already begun its countdown to hardware.

Beneath the surface of that fitness, my tendons were weakening from repetitive overhead lifts without proper recovery. My metabolism was starting to slow, though the military's weight standards didn't account for that. My hormones were beginning their gradual decline, though we never talked about that in a culture where any sign of physical limitation was seen as weakness.

I thought I had time. I thought my determination would carry me through. I thought the pain was temporary.

I was catastrophically wrong about all of it.

This chapter explores the biological shifts that start in your 30s—the same shifts I was ignoring while I proved I wasn't weak. Understanding these changes isn't about bracing for decline. It's about recognizing what's happening so you can respond appropriately—something I failed to do until it was too late.

1.1 The Science of Aging: What Happens to Our Bodies After 30?

Biological Changes

As you navigate your 30s and beyond, you'll notice several physiological changes. One of the first signs is a slower metabolism. This slowdown means your body burns calories at a slower rate, which can lead to weight gain if eating habits remain unchanged. Simultaneously, muscle mass naturally begins to decline, a process known as sarcopenia. This reduction in muscle tissue affects strength and mobility and contributes to the further slowing of your metabolism since muscle burns more calories than fat.

Hormonal fluctuations also play a critical role during this phase. Both men and women experience declines in sex hormones - testosterone and estrogen - which influence not only reproductive health but also impact muscle mass, bone density, and fat distribution. These hormonal changes can alter your physical appearance and affect your overall energy levels and mood, leading to potential challenges in maintaining the same lifestyle you enjoyed in your 20s.

In the military, we were celebrated for muscle mass—until weigh-ins, when suddenly that same muscle counted against us. Many of us would crash diet before fitness tests, losing both fat and muscle just to meet an arbitrary number.

We were unknowingly accelerating the very sarcopenia (age-related muscle loss that makes you weaker and more fragile over time) that would haunt us decades later.

I watched fit colleagues get penalized for muscle while "skinny fat" individuals passed. The system didn't measure health—it measured compliance.

Now, at 58, I'm rebuilding muscle I sacrificed decades ago to "make weight." But it's infinitely harder now, and I can't help but think about all those years I fought against my body's strength instead of honoring it.

Cellular Aging

On a cellular level, aging is marked by the shortening of telomeres and the process of cellular senescence. Telomeres (the protective caps on the ends of your chromosomes—think of them like the plastic tips on shoelaces that keep them from fraying) naturally shorten each time a cell divides. Over time, this shortening can lead to cellular aging and dysfunction, contributing to the aging process throughout the body. Cellular senescence refers to the point at which a cell ceases to divide. While this is a protective mechanism against cancer (since cancer cells divide uncontrollably), it also means that the regenerative capacity of tissues dimi.nishes.

Antioxidants play a crucial role in combating this cellular damage. These powerful substances, which you can obtain from various fruits and vegetables, help neutralize free radicals - unstable molecules that can cause oxidative stress and damage cells. By maintaining a diet rich in antioxidants, you can help protect your telomeres from premature shortening and reduce the impact of oxidative stress on your cells.

Every time I lifted those 188-pound weapons with only two people, every time I powered through injury without recovery, every time I operated on six weeks of healing when I needed six months— I was accelerating cellular aging at a level I couldn't see.

The oxidative stress from overuse. The inflammation from repeated injuries. The hormonal disruption from crash dieting. All of it was shortening my telomeres, aging me faster than natural aging would.

If I'd understood what was happening at a cellular level, would I have made different choices? I'd like to think so. But the culture I was in didn't leave room for choices. It left room for compliance.

Hormonal Shifts

The hormonal shifts that begin in your 30s can have profound effects on your body. For women, the gradual path to menopause begins with perimenopause, where estrogen levels start to fluctuate unpredictably, affecting menstrual cycles and overall mood stability. For men, the decrease in testosterone can lead to changes in sexual function, mood, and body composition, notably an increase in body fat and a decrease in muscle mass. These shifts can affect not just your physical health but your emotional well-being.

The military's approach to hormonal health? Ignore it until it becomes a medical problem.

There was no accommodation for perimenopause. No recognition that hormonal decline affects performance. No adjustment to fitness standards as we aged. You were expected to perform at 45 the same way you did at 25. I'm not discussing the military's fitness programs or their standards. I imagine they have changed over the years.

When I started experiencing fatigue, irregular cycles, and decreased recovery—none of that was understood hormonally. It was seen as me "getting soft."

Layer bipolar disorder on top—with its own hormonal disruptions, its effects on pain perception during mania, its impact on recovery during depression. The intersection created a perfect storm that neither military nor civilian medicine knew how to address.

Understanding hormonal shifts in your 30s and 40s—and honoring them rather than fighting them—isn't weakness. It's wisdom. It's the wisdom I didn't have when it mattered most.

Preventative Measures

Addressing these biological changes effectively involves a combination of lifestyle adjustments, dietary strategies, and potentially medical interventions. Regular physical activity, particularly strength training, can mitigate muscle loss and help maintain metabolic rate. A balanced diet rich in nutrients, fiber, and antioxidants supports overall cellular health and can help regulate hormonal fluctuations. For some, particularly those experiencing significant symptoms related to hormonal changes, hormone replacement therapy may be a beneficial option to discuss with healthcare providers.

Incorporating these preventative measures into your daily routine can significantly impact how your body ages. By understanding and responding to these changes proactively, you can maintain vitality and health well into your later years.

1.2 Debunking Myths: Separating Aging Facts from Fiction

In any discussion about aging, certain myths persist that can skew both our expectations and our experiences of growing older. These myths can range from benign misconceptions to misleading beliefs that may hinder us from pursuing a healthy and active lifestyle in our later years. Let's address and dismantle some of these common myths with evidence and real-life observations, setting the stage for a more informed and empowered approach to aging.

Myth vs. Reality

One prevalent myth is that "Aging means getting sick." This belief fosters a bleak attitude toward growing older, implying an inevitable decline into illness. However, aging itself is not a disease but rather a natural process. While it's true that our risk for certain conditions increases as we age, it's equally important to recognize that lifestyle choices play a significant role in determining our health outcomes. Studies have proven that a balanced diet, regular physical activity, and not smoking contribute more to health in our senior years than genetic factors. Thus, while we might not have control over the years passing, we certainly have significant control over how we age.

MYTH: "No Pain, No Gain" - If It Doesn't Hurt, You're Not Improving

This was gospel in fitness culture, and it's one of the most damaging myths I carried for decades.

REALITY: Chronic Pain Is Your Body's Distress Signal, Not a Badge of Honor

There's a difference between the temporary discomfort of muscles adapting (productive) and the pain of tissue damage and injury (destructive). I didn't learn to distinguish until it was too late.

I learned this when my right shoulder became so damaged that the rotator cuff was "not salvageable" and I needed reverse total shoulder replacement at 56. All those years of pushing through pain didn't make me stronger. They made me permanently disabled.

Now I know that strategic rest isn't weakness—it's how you build sustainable strength. Now I know that pain is information, not inspiration. Now I know that "no pain, no gain" should be "chronic pain, permanent loss."

But I know this now, with hardware on my shoulder. I wish I'd known it at 30.

Another common saying, "You can't teach an old dog new tricks," underestimates the capacity for learning and growth at any age. Cognitive research has consistently debunked this myth, showing that adults can continue to learn and develop new skills throughout their lives. Engaging in new activities and learning new skills can be beneficial for the brain, helping to maintain cognitive function and delay the onset of degenerative brain diseases. Let me tell you, aging is NOT for the weak-minded

Similarly, the idea that "Aging is depressing" is another myth that can create unnecessary worry. While some individuals may face challenges such as loneliness or chronic illness, aging itself does not automatically lead to depression. Many older adults report better emotional well-being compared to their younger counterparts, thanks to greater life experience and the ability to regulate emotions more effectively. It's crucial to approach aging with a balanced perspective, recognizing potential challenges but also acknowledging the opportunities for continued growth and satisfaction.

Importance of Lifestyle Choices

I know I've said it before, but if there's one element that can greatly influence the quality of our aging process, it's the lifestyle choices we make. Contrary to the fatalistic belief that genetics determines everything, a large body of research suggests that our daily habits and decisions have a profound impact. For instance, maintaining a healthy diet rich in fruits, vegetables, and lean proteins can help mitigate the risk of chronic diseases often associated with aging, such as heart disease, diabetes, and osteoporosis. Regular physical activity strengthens the heart, muscles, and bones, and can improve mood and energy levels, helping us feel younger and more vibrant. Please, before you dismiss this book, know that this is not about fancy diets or gym memberships; implementing complicated routines or setting unrealistic goals. It's about giving you the tools to personalize those lifestyle choices to ones you are comfortable with and therefore will stick to.

Activity Levels

Defying the myth that one should slow down with age, many individuals not only maintain but also start rigorous physical activities well into their older years. Take, for example, senior athletes who compete in marathons or engage in regular strength training. These individuals are living proof that maintaining high activity levels can preserve both physical and mental health. I'm not saying we all need to become marathon runners. Physical activity stimulates the release of endorphins, known as the body's natural painkillers, which can improve mood and reduce feelings of depression. Furthermore, exercise is known for its role in enhancing sleep quality, boosting cognitive function, and providing a sense of community and accomplishment.

Brain Health

Finally, let's challenge the inevitability of cognitive decline with age. The concepts of neuroplasticity and cognitive reserve are vital in understanding how our brains can remain active and adaptable. Neuroplasticity refers to the brain's ability to reorganize itself by forming new neural connections throughout life. This ability means that engaging in mentally stimulating activities can enhance brain function and protect against cognitive decline. Cognitive reserve refers to the mind's resilience to neuropathological damage. Studies have shown that individuals with higher cognitive reserve can better maintain their cognitive abilities despite changes in the brain associated with aging.

By dispelling these tales and choosing a lifestyle that promotes physical, mental, and emotional health, we can all look forward to a future where aging is not feared but accepted as an inevitable opportunity for continued growth and enrichment.

"Belief alone isn't enough—action matters. And one of the most powerful forms of action is prevention."

1.3 Essential Screenings: Your Preventive Health Checklist for Your 30s

Understanding the pivotal role that preventive health screenings play in maintaining long-term well-being cannot be overstated, especially as we navigate the complexities of our 30s. This decade often brings significant life changes—career advancements, family growth, and more—which can shift our focus away from health maintenance. Yet, it is exactly during these years that early screenings can be most beneficial. Detecting potential health issues before symptoms manifest can dramatically alter the course of treatment and prognosis, effectively preventing the escalation of manageable conditions into more severe health challenges. Consequently, embracing a proactive approach to health screenings enhances your quality of life and serves as a crucial investment in your future health.

For individuals in their 30s, several key screenings are recommended to monitor and maintain health. Blood pressure checks are perhaps the most fundamental, as hypertension often develops without symptoms but increases the risk of heart disease and stroke significantly. Regular cholesterol checks are similarly essential, given their role in preventing cardiovascular diseases. Cholesterol levels can be influenced by diet, weight, physical activity, and genetics, and identifying issues early can lead to lifestyle interventions or treatments that mitigate long-term risks. Diabetes screenings are also critical, especially for those with predispositions such as family history or obesity, as early detection allows for dietary adjustments, medication, and monitoring to prevent complications like nerve damage, kidney disease, and vision problems. Additionally, cancer screenings should be considered depending on one's family history and risk factors; for instance, those with a family history of colon cancer may start regular screenings earlier than the standard recommendation.

The frequency of these screenings can vary based on individual risk factors. Generally, blood pressure should be checked at least once a year, but more frequently if there are concerns or if previous readings were elevated. Cholesterol is typically screened every 4–6 years in adults without risk factors, but those with identified risks or a family history of heart disease may require more frequent checks. Diabetes screening frequency should align with one's weight, family history, and other health indicators, with at-risk individuals undergoing testing every 1–3 years. Cancer screenings are more personalized, often dictated by specific guidelines associated with each type of cancer and individual risk assessments.

Navigating healthcare systems to access these screenings can be daunting, yet several strategies can simplify this process. First, establishing a relationship with a primary care physician who can coordinate these screenings and interpret their results is invaluable. They serve as your first point of contact within the healthcare system and can guide you through the often-complex landscape of preventive health. Understanding your health insurance coverage is equally crucial; many insurance plans cover preventive screenings at no extra cost to you, but understanding the specifics of your coverage can help avoid unexpected expenses. For those without insurance or with inadequate coverage, exploring local health clinics and community health centers can provide accessible alternatives.

These centers often offer screenings at reduced costs or on a sliding scale based on income.

Additionally, staying informed about your health rights and the services available to you can empower you to make educated decisions about when and where to receive care. In an age where information is readily available, taking the time to research, ask questions, and advocate for oneself with healthcare providers is crucial. Remember, the goal of these screenings is not just to check a box on a medical form but to provide you with insights into your health that enable proactive, informed decisions about your lifestyle and care.

1.4 Key Nutrients and Supplements for Preventing Early Aging

As we move deeper into adulthood, the focus often shifts from merely sustaining health to actively preventing the early signs of aging. This proactive approach enhances our current quality of life and sets the stage for healthier years ahead. Central to this strategy is the understanding and incorporation of specific nutrients and supplements that battle the early signs of aging. Preventing early aging requires a focus on key nutrients and supplements that support overall health and vitality. Essential vitamins such as C and E act as powerful antioxidants, protecting the skin from oxidative stress and promoting collagen production for firmness and elasticity. Vitamins such as D and B12 play pivotal roles in maintaining cellular and bone health, immune function and overall vitality. Omega-3 fatty acids, found in fish oil and flaxseed, reduce inflammation and play a key role in preserving mental acuity. Minerals like zinc and selenium play roles in cellular repair and immune function. Additionally, supplements like CoQ10 and resveratrol can enhance energy production and combat the signs of aging at the cellular level. By incorporating these nutrients into your diet, you can effectively promote longevity and maintain youthful vigor. Antioxidants are your cellular bodyguards; they combat free radicals, which are unstable molecules that can cause oxidative stress, leading to premature aging and various diseases. Foods rich in antioxidants include berries, dark chocolate, and leafy greens. Integrating these into your diet isn't just beneficial; it's a delicious way to combat aging.

The role of supplements in this aging-prevention arsenal can be significant, but must be approached with caution. Supplements can help bridge the nutritional gaps in our diets, especially when everyday meals might not fully meet our nutritional needs, possibly due to lifestyle constraints or declining nutrient absorption, which is often seen as we age. However, the key is choosing high-quality products. Always opt for supplements that have been tested for purity and come from reputable sources. Likewise, be wary of over-supplementation. Fat-soluble vitamins, for example, can accumulate in the body to toxic levels if taken excessively. It's essential, therefore, to discuss any supplementation plan with a healthcare provider to tailor it to your specific needs, considering both your diet and any medical conditions. This does not mean going to the pharmacy and buying every supplement on the shelf. Incorporating these nutrients into daily meals can be simpler than it sounds. Start by increasing the presence of fatty fish in your diet, aiming for two to three servings per week to enhance your omega-3 fatty acid intake. For antioxidants, focus on diversity: try to include fruits, maybe as shakes and smoothies or other tasty drinks, or vegetables of various colors in every meal, as each color represents different beneficial compounds. Breakfast can be upgraded by adding berries or slices of avocado, while snacks can be swapped for nuts or seeds, both of which are high in vitamin E, another powerful antioxidant. For those struggling with dietary sources of Vitamin B12, particularly vegetarians and vegans, fortified cereals or plant-based milk can be excellent alternatives.

Monitoring how your body responds to these dietary changes and supplements is important. Positive indicators such as increased energy levels, improved mood, and a more vibrant skin appearance can signify that your body is well-nourished and aging healthily. Conversely, symptoms like nausea, headaches, or changes in urine color could suggest nutrient excesses, particularly from fat-soluble vitamins or mineral supplements like iron. Keeping track of your dietary intake and any subsequent physical or emotional changes can be an effective way to discover what works best for your body, providing valuable insights that can help adjust your nutritional plan for optimal health. This practice not only keeps you aligned with your body's needs but also fosters a greater connection to how the foods you eat influence your overall well-being.

Please, don't just go buy supplements without talking to your doctor, especially if you are on pharmaceuticals. Make a list of your meds and a list of the supplements that might be needed so you don't create an adverse reaction.

I almost killed my self on accident when I started taking two new supps on top of my pharma load. I started blacking out while walking. No warning just BOOM! Legs don't work field of view decreasing and then I'm coming to be surrounded by concerned people. Of course, my husband will not let me live down the incident where I almost burned the house down and I had no recollection of the incident. So please, please make sure you read the ingredients. Look for duplications and contraindications. Most medicines do not solve only one problem. They multitask. Like the Diabetes medications Mounjaro or wegovy or ozempic, now being used for weight loss. Or Viagra which was originally used as a heart medicine. It behooves you to do your due diligence and a little research.

1.5 Mental Milestones: Preparing Your Mind for the Decades Ahead

Cultivating Mental Resilience

As we age, our ability to handle stress and adapt to change becomes more pressing. Mental resilience, the capacity to recover quickly from difficulties and adapt to stress, is not an innate trait but a skill that can be developed and strengthened. Techniques such as mindfulness meditation and cognitive behavioral strategies are powerful tools in this endeavor. Mindfulness meditation encourages us to remain present and engaged, reducing the tendency to ruminate on past troubles or worry about the future. Regular practice can significantly decrease stress and anxiety, fostering a state of calmness that enhances overall well-being. Cognitive behavioral strategies, on the other hand, involve identifying negative thought patterns and actively challenging them. This method not only helps in managing stress but also improves coping mechanisms during challenging times. By integrating these practices into your daily routine, you create a robust framework that supports mental agility and resilience, preparing you to handle life's inevitable changes with grace and strength.

Lifelong Learning

The pursuit of lifelong learning plays an integral role in maintaining cognitive function and overall mental vitality. Engaging in new learning activities, such as acquiring a new language or picking up a musical instrument, has been shown to enhance neuroplasticity—the brain's ability to form new neural connections. Each new skill learned adds to your repertoire and fortifies your brain against age-related cognitive decline. For instance, learning a new language involves complex cognitive processes involving memory, reasoning, and problem-solving, all of which contribute to greater cognitive reserve—the mind's resistance to damage to the brain. Similarly, learning to play a musical instrument can improve hand-eye coordination, sharpen your ability to concentrate, and increase auditory skills. These activities enrich your life, providing joy and satisfaction while also maintaining the sharpness of your mind.

Social Connections

The impact of social engagement on mental health cannot be overstated. Strong social connections are associated with reduced risk of many health problems, including depression and high blood pressure, and may even influence longevity. As we age, maintaining and broadening social networks becomes essential. Active engagement in social activities can enhance emotional exchanges and support systems, which are crucial for mental health. Strategies to maintain social connections include regular participation in community activities, joining clubs or groups that align with your interests, or volunteering, which also provides a sense of purpose and accomplishment. In the digital age, technology also offers new ways to stay connected with friends and family through social media platforms and communication tools like video calls, making it easier to maintain relationships even over long distances.

Preventing Mental Health Decline

Proactively caring for your mental health involves being vigilant and responsive to the early signs of mental health issues such as depression or anxiety. Recognizing these signs early on is crucial for effective intervention. Symptoms to watch for include persistent sadness or low mood, loss of interest in previously enjoyed activities, withdrawal from social interactions, changes in appetite, and disturbed sleep patterns. If you or someone you know is experiencing these symptoms, it is important to seek professional help. Mental health professionals can provide assessments, support, and treatments that can greatly improve quality of life. Additionally, establishing a routine that includes physical activity, social interaction, and mental challenges can prevent the onset or worsening of symptoms. It's also beneficial to create a supportive environment that encourages open discussions about mental health, reducing stigma and promoting a more proactive approach to mental wellness.

As we advance in years, the landscape of our lives continues to evolve. Embracing these changes with a proactive mindset equipped with effective strategies for mental resilience, continuous learning, social engagement, and mental health care can transform the latter decades into a period of rich fulfillment and vibrant health. This proactive approach enhances our quality of life and sets a positive example for generations to follow, proving that mental vitality can indeed flourish at any age.

Chapter 2: Nutritional Strategies for Ageless Health

As you step into your 40s, a decade often marked by increased professional responsibilities and perhaps growing family obligations, it becomes even more crucial to pay attention to your diet. The choices you make at the dining table can either fuel you through this bustling period or leave you struggling to keep up. If you've noticed that your body isn't quite as forgiving as it was in your 20s or even your 30s, you're not alone. Metabolic rates decline, and muscle mass decreases, but the good news is, that with the right dietary adjustments, you can revitalize your body and continue to enjoy robust health. This chapter dives deep into the strategic shifts needed in your nutritional plan to optimize your health as you navigate these middle years.

2.1 Adapting Your Diet for Your 40s: What Needs to Change?

Increasing Nutrient Density

As your metabolism slows down, it becomes essential to focus on nutrient-dense foods that provide high nutritional value without excess calories that can lead to weight gain. Nutrient-dense foods are rich in vitamins, minerals, fiber, and other beneficial substances while being relatively low in calories. Leafy greens like spinach and kale, lean proteins such as chicken breast or tofu, and whole grains like quinoa and oatmeal are excellent choices. These foods help manage weight and contribute to the prevention of chronic diseases that can start to appear in your 40s. Incorporating a variety of these foods into your meals ensures that you're not only satiated but also nourished.

Balancing Macronutrients

Understanding and adjusting your macronutrient intake is central during this decade. Protein becomes especially important to combat the natural loss of muscle mass due to aging. Including a source of high-quality protein in every meal supports muscle repair and growth, which in turn helps maintain your metabolic rate. Chicken, fish, legumes, and dairy products are excellent protein sources. Carbohydrates should come from whole grains and vegetables, which provide the energy needed to sustain daily activities while stabilizing blood sugar levels. Healthy fats from sources like avocados, nuts, and seeds are crucial for hormone balance and can help absorb fat-soluble vitamins, which are vital for your overall health.

Hydration Focus

Hydration is another key element that needs special attention as you age. With the years, your body's ability to conserve water decreases, and the sense of thirst may not be as acute. This change makes you more susceptible to dehydration, which can impact everything from cognitive function, skin elasticity, and appearance to joint health. Make a conscious effort to drink fluids throughout the day, not just when you feel thirsty. Incorporating foods with high water content, such as cucumbers, tomatoes, and watermelon, can also help increase your overall fluid intake. Herbal teas and broths are other excellent ways to hydrate and can be especially appealing if you're looking to add variety to your fluid intake.

Dietary Adjustments for Health Conditions

In your 40s, you may become more susceptible to health conditions such as hypertension and type 2 diabetes, which can significantly affect your quality of life. Dietary adjustments can play a powerful role in managing and even reversing these conditions. Reducing sodium intake is necessary for managing blood pressure while balancing carbohydrate intake can help control blood sugar levels. For those dealing with hypertension, incorporating potassium-rich foods like bananas and sweet potatoes can aid in lowering blood pressure. For blood sugar management, focus on low-glycemic foods like lentils and non-starchy vegetables to prevent spikes in blood sugar.

Through these dietary strategies, you not only tackle the challenges that come with aging but also enhance your ability to enjoy these years actively and healthily. Making these adjustments requires mindfulness and commitment, but consider this: the quality of your diet shapes the quality of your life. By choosing nutrient-dense foods, balancing your macronutrients, staying hydrated, and adjusting your diet to meet the needs of your body as it changes, you're setting the stage for a healthier, vibrant future.

2.2 Superfoods for Super Aging: What to Eat to Boost Longevity

When it comes to your diet, you've probably heard the term "superfoods" tossed around quite a bit. But what exactly are these nutritional powerhouses, and why are they so beneficial, especially as you age? Simply put, superfoods are items that offer maximum nutritional benefits for minimal calories. They are packed with vitamins, minerals, antioxidants, and other nutrients that can significantly boost health and longevity. These foods are not just good for you; they're great for you, providing a range of benefits from reducing inflammation to enhancing cognitive function.

Let's break down some of these superfoods and their specific benefits. Berries, for example, are rich in vitamins, soluble fiber, and antioxidants known as anthocyanins. These compounds help reduce inflammation and oxidative stress, conditions linked to chronic diseases such as arthritis and heart disease, and even cognitive decline. Then there are leafy greens like spinach and kale, loaded with vitamins A, C, E, and K, and minerals like iron and calcium. These nutrients support bone health, improve blood glucose control, and may lower the risk of chronic illness. Nuts and seeds, including almonds, walnuts, and flaxseeds, are excellent sources of healthy fats, proteins, and fiber. They not only contribute to heart health but also aid in managing weight as they are highly satiating.

Incorporating these superfoods into your daily meals can be both delicious and simple. Start your day with a smoothie that blends berries, a handful of spinach, and a scoop of protein powder for a nutrient-packed breakfast. For snacks, mix nuts and seeds for a homemade trail mix that's perfect for a quick energy boost. Salads provide a great canvas for various superfoods: toss together mixed greens, colorful berries, and a sprinkle of nuts, then drizzle with a vinaigrette for a tasty and healthful lunch or dinner. These small, easy additions to your diet can make a significant difference in how you feel and function, especially as you navigate the complexities of aging.

However, it's pivotal to address some common myths about superfoods. While these foods are highly nutritious, they are not cure-alls, and relying on any single food group to maintain health and wellness is impractical. The key to a healthy diet is variety and balance. No single food, no matter how "super," can provide all the necessary nutrients your body needs. It's also important to consider the source and quality of superfoods. Opt for organic and locally sourced produce whenever possible to ensure you're getting the highest nutrient content without the pesticides commonly used in conventional farming.

Understanding and integrating superfoods into your diet can have profound effects on your health and well-being. By making these nutrient-rich foods a regular part of your eating habits, you're setting the stage for a healthier, more vibrant middle age and beyond. Remember, the goal is to enjoy an assortment of foods that contribute to your health, pleasure, and overall life satisfaction.

2.3 The Truth About Antioxidants and Aging

In the quest for a life full of vitality and youth, antioxidants emerge as critical allies. Found abundantly in various foods, these compounds play a vital role in combating oxidative stress, a key factor in the aging process and many age-related diseases. Oxidative stress occurs when there are too many free radicals—a type of unstable molecule that the body produces as a response to environmental and other pressures—in the body. These free radicals can damage cells, proteins, and DNA, contributing to aging and diseases such as cancer, cardiovascular disease, and Alzheimer's disease. Antioxidants stabilize these free radicals, thus potentially reducing or even preventing some of the damage they cause.

Scientific research supports the benefits of antioxidants. For example, studies have indicated that antioxidants can help delay the onset of vision loss due to age-related macular degeneration, reduce the risk of cancers and heart diseases, and play a role in preventing neurodegenerative diseases like Parkinson's and Alzheimer's. One such study published in the "Journal of Clinical Pathology" emphasized how oxidative stress leads to cellular damage that contributes to the development and progression of chronic diseases and how dietary antioxidants can combat these effects significantly.

When considering sources of antioxidants, it's essential to recognize both well-known and less common options. Blueberries, strawberries, and raspberries are celebrated for their high antioxidant content. However, lesser-known sources such as artichokes and beans provide a substantial antioxidant punch as well. Artichokes, for instance, are loaded with antioxidants called cynarin and silymarin, which are known for their liver health benefits and ability to promote healthy skin. Beans, on the other hand, contain antioxidants like kaempferol and quercetin, which have been shown to reduce inflammation and support heart health.

The debate between obtaining antioxidants from natural sources versus supplements is significant. While supplements can provide a concentrated dose of antioxidants, they lack the additional nutrients found in whole foods that contribute to overall health. In addition, the absorption and utilization of antioxidants can differ when ingested as a part of a whole food as opposed to a supplement. A food-first approach not only ensures a broader intake of beneficial compounds but also reduces the risk of excessive consumption that can occur with supplements. For instance, excessive amounts of antioxidant supplements like beta-carotene and vitamin E have been linked to health risks, including increased mortality rates in some studies.

Incorporating antioxidants into your diet doesn't have to be a chore; it can be a delightful exploration of flavors. One creative way to boost your antioxidant intake is to use herbs and spices in your cooking. Spices such as turmeric, cinnamon, and cloves are not only high in antioxidants but also add immense flavor and depth to dishes. Similarly, herbs like parsley, basil, and thyme provide bursts of flavor while packing a hefty antioxidant punch. Experimenting with different combinations can make your meals exciting and increase your antioxidant intake.

Another effective strategy is to vary your cooking methods to preserve the antioxidant content of food. While boiling vegetables can cause water-soluble antioxidants like vitamin C and some polyphenols to leach into the water, steaming, blanching, or microwaving vegetables can minimize this loss and enhance the availability of antioxidants. Incorporating a mix of raw and cooked antioxidant-rich foods in your diet can help maximize your intake. For example, enjoying both fresh berries and lightly steamed broccoli can optimize your antioxidant consumption, supporting your health and well-being as you age.

By embracing a diet rich in antioxidants, you can enjoy delicious foods and provide your body with the necessary tools to fight the oxidative stress that contributes to aging and disease. Remember, small changes in how you eat and prepare your food can lead to significant benefits for your health and longevity.

2.4 Easy Meal-Prepping for Busy Mid-Lifers

In the rush of day-to-day life, especially during your 40s when professional and personal demands can peak, maintaining a healthy diet can often fall by the wayside. One strategic solution to this common dilemma is meal prepping, which saves time during your hectic week and ensures that you and your family have consistent access to nutritious meals. This proactive approach to food preparation helps streamline your weekly cooking efforts, reduces the stress of last-minute meal decisions, and can significantly cut down on unhealthy food choices that result from spur-of-the-moment decisions.

Meal prepping involves preparing whole meals or dishes ahead of schedule. It's particularly effective for mid-lifers who are balancing career growth with the dynamic needs of family life. By dedicating a few hours to meal preparation each week, you can create several healthy, ready-to-eat dishes that cater to your nutritional needs without the daily hassle. This method helps in maintaining a balanced diet and reduces the temptation to indulge in less healthy, easily accessible food options. Also, meal prepping can contribute to portion control, which is essential for managing weight, especially as metabolism begins to slow down.

Starting with basic meal-prepping strategies, the most foundational technique is batch cooking. This involves cooking larger quantities of a particular recipe and then dividing it into individual portions to be consumed over several days. For instance, a large pot of chili or a hearty vegetable stew can serve as several meals throughout the week, saving time and energy. Another effective strategy is ingredient prep, which includes washing, cutting, marinating, and storing components like vegetables, proteins, and grains. This makes it easy to assemble meals quickly during the week. Effective storage is crucial in meal prepping, as it ensures that your food remains fresh and tasty. Using airtight containers can prevent spoilage and help maintain flavor, making your meals enjoyable as well as convenient.

Let's illustrate how this might look with a sample meal plan for a week:

- **Monday**: Grilled chicken, quinoa salad, and steamed broccoli.

- **Tuesday**: Stir-fry turkey and vegetables with brown rice.

- **Wednesday**: Lentil soup with a side of mixed greens salad.

- **Thursday**: Baked salmon, sweet potato mash, and grilled asparagus.

- **Friday**: Whole wheat pasta with homemade tomato sauce and a side of sautéed spinach.

Each day features balanced portions of protein, carbohydrates, and vegetables, providing a varied diet that supports nutritional needs without repetitive meals. The key is using versatile ingredients that can be mixed and matched to create different meals, ensuring that your diet remains interesting and diverse.

However, meal prepping does come with its challenges, such as dietary restrictions, lack of inspiration, or differing family preferences. These hurdles can make meal prepping seem less feasible, but there are numerous ways to address these issues effectively. For dietary restrictions, focus on customizable dishes that can be easily adjusted. For example, prepare a base dish like a vegetable stir-fry that can be served with either tofu, chicken, or beef, depending on dietary preferences or restrictions. To overcome a lack of inspiration, keep a recipe diary or use meal planning apps that suggest new and exciting recipes based on your dietary preferences and what you have in your pantry.

Adapting meal prepping to accommodate various taste preferences within a family can also seem daunting. One effective strategy is to involve family members in the meal-planning process. This not only ensures that the meals meet everyone's tastes but also makes meal preparation a shared activity that can relieve some of your workload. Another tip is to prepare basic staples like rice, pasta, or potatoes in bulk, which can then be customized with different sauces, spices, or additional ingredients depending on individual preferences. This approach ensures that everyone enjoys their meals without requiring you to prepare separate dishes from scratch for every meal.

By integrating these meal-prepping strategies into your weekly routine, you make healthy eating more achievable and add an element of ease and efficiency to your daily life. Remember, the goal of meal prepping is not just to ease the burden of daily cooking but to ensure that you and your family enjoy nutritious and satisfying meals that support your health and well-being through your busy midlife years.

2.5 Addressing Nutritional Deficiencies Without Breaking the Bank

Navigating the nutritional needs of midlife doesn't have to strain your wallet. It's possible to address common dietary deficiencies such as vitamin D, magnesium, and potassium without compromising on the quality or variety of your food. These nutrients play pivotal roles in maintaining your health; for instance, vitamin D is crucial for bone health and immune function, magnesium supports muscle and nerve function, and potassium aids in blood pressure regulation. Recognizing the signs of deficiency is key— fatigue, muscle cramps, and general lethargy can often signal low levels of these essential nutrients.

Finding cost-effective sources for these nutrients often means turning to whole foods rather than supplements. For vitamin D, fatty fish like salmon and mackerel offer rich sources, but lesser-known options like mushrooms exposed to sunlight can also boost your intake. For magnesium, look beyond expensive supplements to foods like black beans, whole grains, and dark leafy greens, which are not only affordable but also versatile kitchen staples. Potassium-rich foods like bananas, sweet potatoes, and plain yogurt can be bought in bulk and used in a myriad of recipes, ensuring you get your required intake without overspending.

Leveraging community resources can greatly diminish your food expenses while still allowing you to access fresh, nutrient-rich foods. Local farmers' markets often offer produce at lower costs than grocery stores, and the produce is typically fresher and more nutrient-dense, having been picked at peak ripeness. Community gardens are another excellent resource, offering space to grow your own nutrient-rich foods like tomatoes, peppers, and herbs. Participating in a community garden not only reduces food costs but also enhances your connection to the food you eat, making the act of eating itself more meaningful. Food co-ops, where food costs are shared among members, can also provide access to wholesale prices for healthy, organic products.

Strategic grocery shopping is crucial in maximizing nutritional bang for your buck. Begin by planning your meals around seasonal produce, which is more affordable and nutrient-dense. Buying in bulk can also lead to significant savings, especially for non-perishable items like rice, beans, and nuts. When shopping, compare unit prices to get the best deals and consider store-brand products, which often contain the same nutritional value as higher-priced brand names but at a fraction of the cost. By being mindful of how and where you shop, you can make a significant impact on both your health and your finances.

Through these strategies, you can effectively manage and even improve your nutritional health without imposing a heavy financial burden. This approach not only supports your physical health as you navigate midlife but also ensures that you can enjoy a diverse and nutritious diet that supports your overall well-being.

Transitioning to Holistic Lifestyle Changes

As we close this chapter on nutritional strategies, it's clear that what you put on your plate goes beyond mere sustenance. Intentionally choosing foods rich in necessary nutrients, leveraging community resources, and shopping strategically are all part of a larger commitment to maintaining your health through informed choices. These practices not only ensure that you meet your bodily needs but also foster a deeper connection to your food and your community, enriching your life experience.

In the next chapter, we'll expand beyond the plate and explore how integrating physical activity into your routine can further enhance your well-being. Just as we've navigated the complexities of nutrition, we'll uncover the physical practices that best support your health goals, ensuring that you continue to thrive in every aspect of your life.

2.1 Adapting Your Diet for Your 40s: What Needs to Change?

Increasing Nutrient Density

As your metabolism slows down, it becomes essential to focus on nutrient-dense foods that provide high nutritional value without excess calories that can lead to weight gain. Here's the cruel irony: I know all about nutrient-dense foods. I can recite the benefits of leafy greens and lean proteins and whole grains. I can calculate macros and plan balanced meals.

But for decades, I couldn't actually EAT them consistently because my relationship with food was so damaged by "salad week" and weigh-ins and the constant terror of failing a fitness test.

What "salad week" taught me about food:

- Food is the enemy (it makes you gain weight)

- Eating is a weakness (strong people can go without)

- Your body's hunger signals are lying (ignore them)

- Nutrition doesn't matter, only the number on the scale matters

- Starving yourself for a week is fine as long as you pass the test

What this did to my metabolism:

Every time I crash-dieted before a fitness test, my body adapted by:
- Slowing my metabolic rate to conserve energy
- Becoming more efficient at storing fat when food was available again

- Losing muscle mass along with fat (making future weight loss harder)
- Disrupting my hormones (especially thyroid and cortisol)
- Creating insulin resistance from the yo-yo pattern

By my 40s, my metabolism was so damaged from decades of this pattern that "eating normally" caused weight gain. My body had learned to expect starvation periods and prepared accordingly by holding onto every calorie.

What "nutrient-dense" meant then vs. now:

THEN: "Nutrient-dense" meant "low calorie" - I ate spinach and chicken breast not because they nourished me, but because they had fewer calories than other options. The nutrients were incidental. The goal was just to eat as little as possible while technically "eating healthy."

NOW: "Nutrient-dense" actually means nourishing my body. Eating spinach provides iron and vitamins. Eating chicken because my muscles need protein to rebuild. Eating whole grains because my brain needs sustained energy.

This shift—from "eating to weigh less" to "eating to be nourished"—required years of work. It's not just knowledge. It's undoing decades of disordered thinking.

If you're reading this and you recognize the pattern—the crash diets, the fear of food, the scale controlling your choices—know that it's possible to rebuild a healthy relationship with nutrition. But it requires more than just knowing what foods are healthy. It requires healing your relationship with eating itself.

Nutrient-dense foods are rich in vitamins, minerals, fiber, and other beneficial substances while being relatively low in calories. Leafy greens like spinach and kale, lean proteins such as chicken breast or tofu, and whole grains like quinoa and oatmeal are excellent choices. These foods help manage weight and contribute to the prevention of chronic diseases that can start to appear in your 40s. Incorporating a variety of these foods into your meals ensures that you're not only satiated but also nourished.

Balancing Macronutrients

Understanding and adjusting your macronutrient intake is central during this decade. Protein becomes especially important to combat the natural loss of muscle mass due to aging. Including a source of high-quality protein in every meal supports muscle repair and growth, which in turn helps maintain your metabolic rate. Chicken, fish, legumes, and dairy products are excellent protein sources. Carbohydrates should come from whole grains and vegetables, which provide the energy needed to sustain daily activities while stabilizing blood sugar levels. Healthy fats from sources like avocados, nuts, and seeds are crucial for hormone balance and can help absorb fat-soluble vitamins, which are vital for your overall health.

The military taught me to fear carbohydrates. Carbs make you fat, they said. Carbs make you fail weigh-ins. Cut carbs and you'll make weight.

So I did. For years, I severely restricted carbohydrates, especially before fitness tests. I'd eat nothing but protein and vegetables, eliminating all grains, fruits, and even starchy vegetables.

What actually happened:

- I lost weight initially (mostly water and muscle, not fat)

- My energy plummeted (my brain literally runs on glucose from carbs)

- My workouts suffered (no glycogen stores for muscle fuel)

- I became irritable and foggy (low-carb brain fog is real)

- I gained the weight back immediately when I ate normally again

This pattern repeated for DECADES. Cut carbs. Lose weight. Pass the test. Resume eating. Gain weight back. Repeat.

Each cycle made it worse. My body became more resistant. My metabolism slowed further. The amount I had to restrict increased each time to get the same result.

Now, I understand macronutrient balance differently:

Protein: Essential for maintaining muscle mass (which I desperately need after all the muscle I sacrificed to "make weight"). I need MORE protein now than I did in my 20s, not less.

Carbohydrates: Not the enemy. My brain needs them. My muscles need them. The quality matters (whole grains vs. refined sugars), but eliminating them entirely was sabotage, not strategy.

Fats: Critical for hormone production (which affects EVERYTHING from mood to metabolism to recovery). All those years I ate "fat-free" everything, I was starving my hormones and wondering why I felt terrible.

The shift from restriction to balance:

I don't "cut" anything anymore. I don't "eliminate" food groups. I don't panic about carbs or fat.

I eat protein because my damaged shoulders need it to rebuild what little function they have left. I eat carbs because my brain and energy levels need them. I eat healthy fats because my hormones need them.

This feels revolutionary after decades of restriction. And it's still hard sometimes—the voice that says "that's too many carbs" or "you shouldn't eat fat" is loud and persistent.

But I'm learning. At 58. After decades of damage. If I'd understood macronutrient BALANCE instead of macronutrient FEAR in my 30s, my metabolism wouldn't be fighting me now.

Hydration Focus

Hydration is another key element that needs special attention as you age. With the years, your body's ability to conserve water decreases, and the sense of thirst may not be as acute. This change makes you more susceptible to dehydration, which can impact everything from cognitive function, skin elasticity, and appearance to joint health. Make a conscious effort to drink fluids throughout the day, not just when you feel thirsty. Incorporating foods with high water content, such as cucumbers, tomatoes, and watermelon, can also help increase your overall fluid intake. Herbal teas and broths are other excellent ways to hydrate and can be especially appealing if you're looking to add variety to your fluid intake.

During "salad week," we'd also manipulate our water intake. Drink tons of water early in the week (to "flush out" water weight), then restrict fluids the day before weigh-in to drop those last few pounds of water weight.

This is textbook eating disorder behavior. But in the military, it was standard practice.

What chronic dehydration did:

- Made me constantly exhausted

- Caused headaches and difficulty concentrating

- Compromised my physical performance (the very thing we were trying to optimize)

- Damaged my kidneys over time

- Made my skin look terrible

- Contributed to joint pain (cartilage needs water)

The psychological damage:

Even now, I sometimes "forget" to drink water. Not because I'm actually forgetting—because decades of deliberately dehydrating myself created a pattern where thirst signals got ignored or suppressed.

I have to consciously remind myself: "You're allowed to drink water. Water isn't making you fail. Your body NEEDS water."

This sounds absurd when written out. But it's real. Decades of manipulating water intake for weigh-ins damaged my relationship with something as basic as hydration.

Now:

I keep a water bottle with me always. I track my intake (not to restrict, but to ensure I'm getting ENOUGH). I drink herbal tea, eat water-rich foods, and consciously rehydrate.

But I'm still undoing damage from my 20s and 30s. My joints are already compromised from injuries and surgeries—chronic dehydration during those crucial healing periods probably made it worse.

If you're manipulating your hydration for weight control, STOP. The temporary drop in scale weight isn't worth the long-term damage to your kidneys, joints, skin, and cognitive function.

Dietary Adjustments for Health Conditions

In your 40s, you may become more susceptible to health conditions such as hypertension and type 2 diabetes, which can significantly affect your quality of life. Dietary adjustments can play a powerful role in managing and even reversing these conditions. Reducing sodium intake is necessary for managing blood pressure while balancing carbohydrate intake can help control blood sugar levels. For those dealing with hypertension, incorporating potassium-rich foods like bananas and sweet potatoes can aid in lowering blood pressure. For blood sugar management, focus on low-glycemic foods like lentils and non-starchy vegetables to prevent spikes in blood sugar.

Through these dietary strategies, you not only tackle the challenges that come with aging but also enhance your ability to enjoy these years actively and healthily. Making these adjustments requires mindfulness and commitment, but consider this: the quality of your diet shapes the quality of your life. By choosing nutrient-dense foods, balancing your macronutrients, staying hydrated, and adjusting your diet to meet the needs of your body as it changes, you're setting the stage for a healthier, vibrant future.

2.2 Superfoods for Super Aging: What to Eat to Boost Longevity

When it comes to your diet, you've probably heard the term "superfoods" tossed around quite a bit. But what exactly are these nutritional powerhouses, and why are they so beneficial, especially as you age? Simply put, superfoods are items that offer maximum nutritional benefits for minimal calories. They are packed with vitamins, minerals, antioxidants, and other nutrients that can significantly boost health and longevity. These foods are not just good for you; they're great for you, providing a range of benefits from reducing inflammation to enhancing cognitive function.

Here's what's darkly funny about "superfoods": I was eating them during "salad week." Spinach, kale, berries—all the nutrient-dense foods recommended for healthy aging.

But I wasn't eating them for their nutrients. I was eating them because they were low-calorie. The antioxidants and vitamins were incidental. I was starving my body while technically "eating healthy."

The difference between eating superfoods and being nourished:

EATING SUPERFOODS WHILE STARVING:

- A giant salad with no dressing, no protein, no fats

- Raw vegetables with nothing else

- Berries as your only food for the day

- Enough volume to feel full, not enough calories to function

ACTUALLY BEING NOURISHED:

- Leafy greens WITH healthy fats (so you absorb the fat-soluble vitamins)

- Berries WITH protein (to stabilize blood sugar)

- Whole meals that include superfoods as PART of balanced nutrition

- Enough total calories to support your body's actual needs

- During "salad week," I was technically eating "superfoods" while creating massive nutritional deficits that damaged my metabolism, hormones, and muscle mass.

The nutrients in those foods couldn't help me because I wasn't eating ENOUGH of anything.

Now:

I still eat all these superfoods. But now they're part of ADEQUATE nutrition, not restriction masquerading as health. I eat berries with yogurt and nuts. I eat leafy greens with salmon and avocado. I eat enough.

This is harder than it sounds after decades of "salad week" mentality. Some days I still have to consciously give myself permission to eat more than a giant pile of vegetables.

But I'm learning that "superfoods" only work if you're actually nourished, not starving.

Let's break down some of these superfoods and their specific benefits. Berries, for example, are rich in vitamins, soluble fiber, and antioxidants known as anthocyanins. These compounds help reduce inflammation and oxidative stress, conditions linked to chronic diseases such as arthritis and heart disease, and even cognitive decline. Then there are leafy greens like spinach and kale, loaded with vitamins A, C, E, and K, and minerals like iron and calcium. These nutrients support bone health, improve blood glucose control, and may lower the risk of chronic illness. Nuts and seeds, including almonds, walnuts, and flaxseeds, are excellent sources of healthy fats, proteins, and fiber. They not only contribute to heart health but also aid in managing weight as they are highly satiating.

Incorporating these superfoods into your daily meals can be both delicious and simple. Start your day with a smoothie that blends berries, a handful of spinach, and a scoop of protein powder for a nutrient-packed breakfast. For snacks, mix nuts and seeds for a homemade trail mix that's perfect for a quick energy boost. Salads provide a great canvas for various superfoods: toss together mixed greens, colorful berries, and a sprinkle of nuts, then drizzle with a vinaigrette for a tasty and healthful lunch or dinner. These small, easy additions to your diet can make a significant difference in how you feel and function, especially as you navigate the complexities of aging.

However, it's pivotal to address some common myths about superfoods. While these foods are highly nutritious, they are not cure-alls, and relying on any single food group to maintain health and wellness is impractical. The key to a healthy diet is variety and balance. No single food, no matter how "super," can provide all the necessary nutrients your body needs. It's also important to consider the source and quality of superfoods. Opt for organic and locally sourced produce whenever possible to ensure you're getting the highest nutrient content without the pesticides commonly used in conventional farming.

Understanding and integrating superfoods into your diet can have profound effects on your health and well-being. By making these nutrient-rich foods a regular part of your eating habits, you're setting the stage for a healthier, more vibrant middle age and beyond. Remember, the goal is to enjoy an assortment of foods that contribute to your health, pleasure, and overall life satisfaction.

2.3 The Truth About Antioxidants and Aging

In the quest for a life full of vitality and youth, antioxidants emerge as critical allies. Found abundantly in various foods, these compounds play a vital role in combating oxidative stress, a key factor in the aging process and many age-related diseases. Oxidative stress occurs when there are too many free radicals—a type of unstable molecule that the body produces as a response to environmental and other pressures—in the body. These free radicals can damage cells, proteins, and DNA, contributing to aging and diseases such as cancer, cardiovascular disease, and Alzheimer's disease. Antioxidants stabilize these free radicals, thus potentially reducing or even preventing some of the damage they cause.

Scientific research supports the benefits of antioxidants. For example, studies have indicated that antioxidants can help delay the onset of vision loss due to age-related macular degeneration, reduce the risk of cancers and heart diseases, and play a role in preventing neurodegenerative diseases like Parkinson's and Alzheimer's. One such study published in the "Journal of Clinical Pathology" emphasized how oxidative stress leads to cellular damage that contributes to the development and progression of chronic diseases and how dietary antioxidants can combat these effects significantly.

When considering sources of antioxidants, it's essential to recognize both well-known and less common options. Blueberries, strawberries, and raspberries are celebrated for their high antioxidant content. However, lesser-known sources such as artichokes and beans provide a substantial antioxidant punch as well. Artichokes, for instance, are loaded with antioxidants called cynarin and silymarin, which are known for their liver health benefits and ability to promote healthy skin. Beans, on the other hand, contain antioxidants like kaempferol and quercetin, which have been shown to reduce inflammation and support heart health.

The debate between obtaining antioxidants from natural sources versus supplements is significant. While supplements can provide a concentrated dose of antioxidants, they lack the additional nutrients found in whole foods that contribute to overall health. In addition, the absorption and utilization of antioxidants can differ when ingested as a part of a whole food as opposed to a supplement. A food-first approach not only ensures a broader intake of beneficial compounds but also reduces the risk of excessive consumption that can occur with supplements. For instance, excessive amounts of antioxidant supplements like beta-carotene and vitamin E have been linked to health risks, including increased mortality rates in some studies.

Incorporating antioxidants into your diet doesn't have to be a chore; it can be a delightful exploration of flavors. One creative way to boost your antioxidant intake is to use herbs and spices in your cooking. Spices such as turmeric, cinnamon, and cloves are not only high in antioxidants but also add immense flavor and depth to dishes. Similarly, herbs like parsley, basil, and thyme provide bursts of flavor while packing a hefty antioxidant punch. Experimenting with different combinations can make your meals exciting and increase your antioxidant intake.

Another effective strategy is to vary your cooking methods to preserve the antioxidant content of food. While boiling vegetables can cause water-soluble antioxidants like vitamin C and some polyphenols to leach into the water, steaming, blanching, or microwaving vegetables can minimize this loss and enhance the availability of antioxidants. Incorporating a mix of raw and cooked antioxidant-rich foods in your diet can help maximize your intake. For example, enjoying both fresh berries and lightly steamed broccoli can optimize your antioxidant consumption, supporting your health and well-being as you age.

By embracing a diet rich in antioxidants, you can enjoy delicious foods and provide your body with the necessary tools to fight the oxidative stress that contributes to aging and disease. Remember, small changes in how you eat and prepare your food can lead to significant benefits for your health and longevity.

2.4 Easy Meal-Prepping for Busy Mid-Lifers

In the rush of day-to-day life, especially during your 40s when professional and personal demands can peak, maintaining a healthy diet can often fall by the wayside. One strategic solution to this common dilemma is meal prepping, which saves time during your hectic week and ensures that you and your family have consistent access to nutritious meals. This proactive approach to food preparation helps streamline your weekly cooking efforts, reduces the stress of last-minute meal decisions, and can significantly cut down on unhealthy food choices that result from spur-of-the-moment decisions.

Meal prepping involves preparing whole meals or dishes ahead of time. It's particularly effective for mid-lifers who are balancing career growth with the dynamic needs of family life. By dedicating a few hours to meal preparation each week, you can create several healthy, ready-to-eat dishes that cater to your nutritional needs without the daily hassle. This method helps in maintaining a balanced diet and reduces the temptation to indulge in less healthy, easily accessible food options. Also, meal prepping can contribute to portion control, which is essential for managing weight, especially as metabolism begins to slow down.

Starting with basic meal-prepping strategies, the most foundational technique is batch cooking. This involves cooking larger quantities of a particular recipe and then dividing it into individual portions to be consumed over several days. For instance, a large pot of chili or a hearty vegetable stew can serve as several meals throughout the week, saving time and energy. Another effective strategy is ingredient prep, which includes washing, cutting, marinating, and storing components like vegetables, proteins, and grains. This makes it easy to assemble meals quickly during the week. Effective storage is crucial in meal prepping, as it ensures that your food remains fresh and tasty. Using airtight containers can prevent spoilage and help maintain flavor, making your meals enjoyable as well as convenient.

Let's illustrate how this might look with a sample meal plan for a week:

- **Monday**: Grilled chicken, quinoa salad, and steamed broccoli.

- **Tuesday**: Stir-fry turkey and vegetables with brown rice.

- **Wednesday**: Lentil soup with a side of mixed greens salad.

- **Thursday**: Baked salmon, sweet potato mash, and grilled asparagus.

- **Friday**: Whole wheat pasta with homemade tomato sauce and a side of sautéed spinach.

Each day features balanced portions of protein, carbohydrates, and vegetables, providing a varied diet that supports nutritional needs without repetitive meals. The key is using versatile ingredients that can be mixed and matched to create different meals, ensuring that your diet remains interesting and diverse.

However, meal prepping does come with its challenges, such as dietary restrictions, lack of inspiration, or differing family preferences. These hurdles can make meal prepping seem less feasible, but there are numerous ways to address these issues effectively. For dietary restrictions, focus on customizable dishes that can be easily adjusted. For example, prepare a base dish like a vegetable stir-fry that can be served with either tofu, chicken, or beef, depending on dietary preferences or restrictions. To overcome a lack of inspiration, keep a recipe diary or use meal planning apps that suggest new and exciting recipes based on your dietary preferences and what you have in your pantry.

Adapting meal prepping to accommodate various taste preferences within a family can also seem daunting. One effective strategy is to involve family members in the meal-planning process. This not only ensures that the meals meet everyone's tastes but also makes meal preparation a shared activity that can relieve some of your workload. Another tip is to prepare basic staples like rice, pasta, or potatoes in bulk, which can then be customized with different sauces, spices, or additional ingredients depending on individual preferences. This approach ensures that everyone enjoys their meals without requiring you to prepare separate dishes from scratch for every meal.

By integrating these meal-prepping strategies into your weekly routine, you make healthy eating more achievable and add an element of ease and efficiency to your daily life. Remember, the goal of meal prepping is not just to ease the burden of daily cooking but to ensure that you and your family enjoy nutritious and satisfying meals that support your health and well-being through your busy midlife years.

The sample meal plan you just read—grilled chicken, quinoa, vegetables, salmon, sweet potatoes—is exactly what I SHOULD have been eating in my 30s and 40s.

But I wasn't. Here's what I was actually eating:

Week 1-3 of the month: Relatively normal eating (though always watching calories)

Week 4 (before fitness test): "Salad week"

- Monday: Salad with no dressing, black coffee

- Tuesday: Grilled chicken (plain), steamed vegetables, water

- Wednesday: Salad, maybe some tuna

- Thursday: Barely eating (test is Friday)

- Friday: NOTHING before weigh-in

- Friday afternoon (after passing): Binge eating everything I'd denied myself

This pattern every single month for YEARS.

What this did:

- Prevented my body from ever establishing a stable metabolism
- Created binge-restrict cycles (classic eating disorder pattern)
- Made my body afraid of starvation (leading to increased fat storage)
- Destroyed my relationship with food
- Made "meal planning" impossible because I couldn't trust myself around food

The psychological damage of meal planning when you have disordered eating:

Normal people's meal plan to: save time, eat healthier, manage budget, and reduce decision fatigue.

People with eating disorder histories plan to: control intake, restrict calories, avoid "dangerous" foods, and create rigid rules that feel safe.

I'm STILL working on this. When I meal plan now, I have to actively fight the urge to:

- Make every meal as low-calorie as possible
- Plan the same "safe" meals over and over
- Skip meals or plan tiny portions
- Avoid any "scary" foods

What healthy meal planning looks like for me now:

- Variety (not the same "safe" chicken and vegetables every day)

- Adequate portions (not restriction portions)

- Including foods I enjoy (not just "allowed" foods)

- Flexibility (not rigid rules that feel like punishment)

But this is HARD. After decades of weaponizing meal planning as a restriction tool, using it as an actual health tool requires constant conscious effort.

If you're meal planning from a place of fear or restriction, it's not really health—it's a diet in disguise. True meal planning for health includes adequacy, variety, and flexibility.

2.5 Addressing Nutritional Deficiencies Without Breaking the Bank

Navigating the nutritional needs of midlife doesn't have to strain your wallet. It's possible to address common dietary deficiencies such as vitamin D, magnesium, and potassium without compromising on the quality or variety of your food. These nutrients play pivotal roles in maintaining your health; for instance, vitamin D is crucial for bone health and immune function, magnesium supports muscle and nerve function, and potassium aids in blood pressure regulation. Recognizing the signs of deficiency is key— fatigue, muscle cramps, and general lethargy can often signal low levels of these essential nutrients.

Finding cost-effective sources for these nutrients often means turning to whole foods rather than supplements. For vitamin D, fatty fish like salmon and mackerel offer rich sources, but lesser-known options like mushrooms exposed to sunlight can also boost your intake. For magnesium, look beyond expensive supplements to foods like black beans, whole grains, and dark leafy greens, which are not only affordable but also versatile kitchen staples. Potassium-rich foods like bananas, sweet potatoes, and plain yogurt can be bought in bulk and used in a myriad of recipes, ensuring you get your required intake without overspending.

Leveraging community resources can greatly diminish your food expenses while still allowing you to access fresh, nutrient-rich foods. Local farmers' markets often offer produce at lower costs than grocery stores, and the produce is typically fresher and more nutrient-dense, having been picked at peak ripeness. Community gardens are another excellent resource, offering space to grow your own nutrient-rich foods like tomatoes, peppers, and herbs. Participating in a community garden not only reduces food costs but also enhances your connection to the food you eat, making the act of eating itself more meaningful. Food co-ops, where food costs are shared among members, can also provide access to wholesale prices for healthy, organic products.

Strategic grocery shopping is crucial in maximizing nutritional bang for your buck. Begin by planning your meals around seasonal produce, which is more affordable and nutrient-dense. Buying in bulk can also lead to significant savings, especially for non-perishable items like rice, beans, and nuts. When shopping, compare unit prices to get the best deals and consider store-brand products, which often contain the same nutritional value as higher-priced brand names but at a fraction of the cost. By being mindful of how and where you shop, you can make a significant impact on both your health and your finances.

Through these strategies, you can effectively manage and even improve your nutritional health without imposing a heavy financial burden. This approach not only supports your physical health as you navigate midlife but also ensures that you can enjoy a diverse and nutritious diet that supports your overall well-being.

You know what creates nutritional deficiencies faster than anything?

Chronic restriction. Yo-yo dieting. "Salad week." The eating patterns I maintained for decades.

My nutritional deficiencies at 58:

- Vitamin D (partly from inadequate intake during restriction periods)

- B vitamins (especially B12, from avoiding meat during "diet" phases)

- Iron (from restricting red meat and pairing iron-rich foods with calcium, which blocks absorption)

- Omega-3 fatty acids (from years of "low-fat" eating)

- Magnesium (from not eating enough nuts, seeds, and whole grains during restriction)

- Calcium (despite drinking milk, because I wasn't absorbing it properly due to vitamin D deficiency and chronic stress)

These deficiencies contributed to:

- Chronic fatigue

- Muscle weakness (on top of my shoulder damage)

- Poor bone density

- Mood issues (in addition to bipolar disorder)

- Slow injury recovery

- Weakened immune system

The bitter irony:

I created these deficiencies while trying to be "healthy." While eating salads and lean protein and exercising religiously. Because I was doing all of it from a foundation of restriction and fear, not nourishment.

Now:

I take supplements (vitamin D, B-complex, magnesium, omega-3). But I also EAT enough food to actually absorb them. I eat fatty fish. I eat nuts and seeds. I eat full-fat dairy. I eat red meat occasionally.

This still feels transgressive sometimes. The voice that says "that's too much fat" or "you shouldn't eat that many calories" is loud.

But my deficiencies are slowly improving. My energy is better. My mood is more stable. My body is finally getting what it needed all along.

If you're addressing nutritional deficiencies:

Make sure you're eating ENOUGH total food for your body to absorb the nutrients. All the supplements in the world won't help if you're chronically under-eating or if your eating patterns are too restrictive to support absorption.

Addressing deficiencies isn't just about adding supplements. It's about adequate, consistent, varied nutrition. It's about NOURISHING yourself, not just technically "eating healthy" while starving.

Transitioning to Holistic Lifestyle Changes

As we close this chapter on nutritional strategies, it's clear that what you put on your plate goes beyond mere sustenance.

Intentionally choosing foods rich in necessary nutrients, leveraging community resources, and shopping strategically are all part of a larger commitment to maintaining your health through informed choices. These practices not only ensure that you meet your bodily needs but also foster a deeper connection to your food and your community, enriching your life experience.

In the next chapter, we'll expand beyond the plate and explore how integrating physical activity into your routine can further enhance your well-being. Just as we've navigated the complexities of nutrition, we'll uncover the physical practices that best support your health goals, ensuring that you continue to thrive in every aspect of your life.

Chapter 3: Physical Wellness and Exercise

I can't lift my own luggage anymore.

That sentence runs through my head every time I travel, every time I see someone effortlessly hoist a suitcase, every time I have to ask a stranger for help with something that weighs less than those 25-pound items I recrated 3,000 times in one day.

I can't carry groceries without multiple trips. I can't reach the overhead shelves without wincing. I can't open jars sometimes. I can't do push-ups. I can't lift my grandchildren. I can't do dozens of ordinary tasks I once did without thinking.

At 58, I live in a body that has betrayed its promises. This is what "no pain, no gain" brought me: premature dependence.

This isn't natural aging. This is accelerated deterioration from treating your body as a tool to be used until it breaks.

The fear of dependence isn't abstract for me. It's my daily reality. Every time I need help with a physical task. Every time I have to modify or skip an activity. Every time I realize there's something my body simply CAN'T do anymore.

This chapter is about physical wellness and exercise. But it's also about the truth those words don't tell: that fitness culture can steal your independence decades before you should lose it.

3.1 Tailoring Your Fitness Regime as You Age

Assessing Current Fitness Levels

Before diving into new exercise routines, it's critical to gauge where you stand physically. This initial assessment isn't about setting benchmarks for competitions but about understanding your body's current state. Start by evaluating your cardiovascular health, flexibility, balance, and strength. Simple tests, like seeing how long you can hold a stretch or how many sit-ups or push-ups you can do comfortably, provide a practical measure of your fitness. Tools such as a step tracker or a heart rate monitor can also offer insights into your cardiovascular and overall health. Remember, the goal here is not to judge yourself but to gather baseline data that will inform the exercise choices you make. This careful approach helps in setting realistic goals and avoiding injuries, ensuring that your fitness journey is both safe and enjoyable.

Here's what my assessment looks like at 58:

Cardiovascular: Decent. I can walk, maintain conversation, heart rate recovers reasonably.

Flexibility: Limited by shoulder hardware. The range of motion in the right arm is permanently restricted to 140 degrees instead of 180. Some poses are impossible.

Balance: Compromised when using the right arm for support. The body compensates, but compensation creates imbalances.

Strength: Upper body profoundly limited. Can't do standard push-ups. Can't pull myself up. Can't lift heavy overhead. Hardware has mechanical limitations that willpower can't overcome.

This honest assessment is what I should have done at 30. Not compared to external standards, but to what my body actually could sustain.

Customizing Exercise Plans

With your current fitness level in mind, the next step is to tailor your exercise regimen. This customization should consider any existing health conditions—like arthritis or heart disease—that might affect your ability to perform certain exercises. For instance, if you have joint issues, you might focus on low-impact exercises such as swimming or cycling rather than jogging or jumping rope. Age-related considerations, such as reduced bone density or decreased muscle mass, should also guide the intensity and type of exercise you include in your routine. For modifications, if standard squats are too strenuous, a chair squat can be an effective alternative, providing similar benefits without the stress on your knees and back. Engaging with a fitness professional can be invaluable here. They can provide personalized advice that aligns with your health status, fitness level, and personal goals, ensuring that your regimen is not only effective but also sustainable.

Military Fitness (Then):

- Push-ups until failure

- Heavy overhead presses

- "Three-man" lifts with two people

- No rest days (rest was weakness)

- Pain was progress

Sustainable Fitness (Now):

- Wall push-ups (not floor)

- No overhead work

- Resistance bands instead of weights

- Scheduled rest days

- Pain is a signal to stop

The shift required completely redefining exercise. Not about proving capability, but maintaining independence.

What I CAN'T do:

- Overhead presses
- Floor push-ups
- Pull-ups
- Certain yoga poses
- Carry heavy items

What I CAN do (modified):

- Wall push-ups

- Resistance band work

- Pilates (carefully modified)

- Walking

- Core work

The mental shift: accepting I'll never do standard push-ups again. Those capabilities are gone permanently.

This is dependence: relying on modifications, adaptations, and workarounds. My plan isn't customized by preference—it's dictated by permanent limitations from not customizing when it mattered.

Importance of Professional Guidance

While self-guided exercises have their place, the expertise of fitness professionals can be a game-changer, especially as you age. These experts can offer guidance on the nuances of exercise mechanics and how to adapt them to benefit your specific needs. They can also help you navigate through the myriad of workout trends and fitness advice that floods our media, choosing what best suits your needs. Whether it's a personal trainer at your gym or a physical therapist, their trained eyes can spot potential issues in your form or program that you might overlook, which could prevent injuries. Furthermore, they can keep your routine dynamic and engaging, helping you push past plateaus and continue to make gains in your strength, flexibility, and endurance. Having said that, you may not want the extra expense. To this end, there are many options on the internet that can help bridge that gap. YouTube is an excellent source for many how-tos.

Feedback and Adjustment

Maintaining an effective exercise routine is not a 'set it and forget it' deal; it requires ongoing tweaks and reviews. This is where regular feedback, either self-generated or from your fitness coach, becomes crucial. Keep a journal or log of your workouts and how you feel during and after them. Note any pain, discomfort, or fatigue that goes beyond normal post-workout tiredness. Use this log to adjust your exercise intensity, duration, and form. Regular re-assessments every few months can help you track your progress and make informed decisions about scaling up or modifying your activities. This kind of attentive management of your fitness regimen supports not just physical health but adapts seamlessly to your evolving lifestyle needs, keeping you active and injury-free as you age.

The secret to maintaining physical wellness and vitality through the years lies in this ongoing dialogue with your body, where you listen and adapt. By embracing a tailored, thoughtful approach to exercise, you build more than muscle or stamina; you cultivate a sustainable practice that supports your well-being through every season of life.

3.2 The Role of Yoga and Pilates in Maintaining Flexibility

The gentle yet profound practices of yoga and Pilates stand out as beacons for those navigating the complexities of aging. These practices offer more than just physical benefits. These disciplines extend their reach into the realms of mental clarity and emotional stability, making them ideal for integrating into your regular fitness regimen, especially as flexibility and joint health become paramount in later years. Let's explore how these practices enhance not only your body's elasticity but also fortify your mind and spirit, ensuring a holistic approach to health and well-being as you age.

Flexibility is more than the ability to touch your toes; it is a crucial component of overall fitness that affects everything from your mobility to your balance. As muscles and joints age, they naturally lose some of their elasticity, range of motion, and fluidity, making daily activities more challenging and increasing the risk of injuries. Yoga and Pilates address these issues head-on by gently stretching and strengthening the muscles, which in turn helps to maintain the lubrication and health of your joints. Regular practice can lead to significant improvements in how your body moves and feels. For instance, poses like the Pilates 'Saw' stretch your back, shoulders, and hamstrings, all while improving spinal rotation. Similarly, yoga poses like 'Pigeon' and 'Butterfly' focus on opening the hips, which can greatly enhance lower body flexibility and reduce the strain on your knees and back.

The benefits of these practices, however, transcend the physical. Both yoga and Pilates are renowned for fostering an unparalleled mind-body connection. This holistic approach does not just involve executing movements; it encompasses an awareness of breathing, an alignment of posture, and a focus on movements that engage both body and mind. This mindful practice can significantly reduce stress levels, as the deep, controlled breathing inherent to both disciplines increases the supply of oxygen to your brain, promoting a sense of calm and relaxation. Furthermore, the concentration required to perform these exercises can enhance your mindfulness, which in turn can lead to improved focus and mental clarity in other areas of your life. This mental engagement is a form of cognitive exercise that helps to keep your mind sharp and alert.

Adapting yoga and Pilates for those who are older or have limited mobility is straightforward, thanks to the inherent flexibility of these practices. Many poses and exercises can be modified to accommodate your specific needs. For example, if balance is a concern, yoga poses can be performed with the support of a chair or against a wall. Pilates exercises can be adapted by reducing the range of motion or by using props like bands or balls to aid movement and reduce strain. These modifications ensure that you can enjoy the benefits of these practices safely, regardless of your physical condition.

I came to Pilates at 58, after surgery, after my career ended, after decades of destruction. Not as an athlete, but as a disabled person seeking to rebuild.

And it saved me.

What Pilates can't fix:

- The hardware The hard wire
- Limited range of motion
- Chronic pain
- Tasks I'll never do again

What Pilates HAS rebuilt:

- Core strength supporting my shoulder
- Better posture reduces pain
- Flexibility in areas not permanently limited
- Mind-body awareness
- Ability to distinguish productive challenge from destructive pain

- Small daily tasks I'd lost

- Sense that improvement is still possible

The irony: decades of "hardcore" fitness destroyed me. "Gentle" Pilates is rebuilding me.

If I'd done Pilates in my 30s—the controlled movements, proper mechanics, modifications—I might still have working shoulders.

Incorporating yoga(not so much) and Pilates into your regular fitness schedule can be both rewarding and enjoyable. If you are new to these practices, starting at home can be a great way to familiarize yourself with the basic movements. Numerous online platforms offer beginner classes that guide you step-by-step through each pose or exercise. Alternatively, enrolling in a class at a local studio can provide you with the guidance of a knowledgeable instructor who can offer immediate feedback and adjustments. Classes also offer the added benefit of community, allowing you to connect with others who share your interests in maintaining health and vitality. Whether you choose to practice at home or in a studio, aim to integrate these exercises into your routine at least two to three times a week. This regular practice can significantly enhance your flexibility, balance, and overall well-being, making yoga and Pilates invaluable allies in your quest for a healthy and active life as you age.

3.3 Strength Training: Building Muscle to Combat Aging

When considering the multifaceted approach to aging well, maintaining and even building muscle mass should hold a prominent place in your fitness regimen. Muscle does more than just enhance physical strength and aesthetics; it plays a crucial role in bolstering your metabolism, supporting bone health, and facilitating everyday activities that become increasingly important as you age. As we grow older, our bodies naturally begin to lose muscle mass, a condition known as sarcopenia. This loss can start as early as your

30s and, without intervention, can lead to diminished strength, slower metabolism, and a higher risk of falls and fractures. However, engaging in regular strength training can significantly counteract these effects by preserving and increasing muscle mass and strength.

Furthermore, the benefits of maintaining strong muscles extend beyond the obvious. Increased muscle mass boosts your metabolism, helping your body to burn calories more efficiently, which is particularly beneficial as your metabolic rate naturally declines with age. This can help manage weight and reduce the risk of obesity-related diseases such as type 2 diabetes and heart disease. In addition, strength training is immensely beneficial for bone health. It increases bone density and reduces the risk of osteoporosis, a common issue that particularly affects women post-menopause. Strong muscles also enhance your balance and coordination, reducing the risk of falls, which can be life-altering in your senior years.

Embarking on a strength training program, particularly if you're new to it, can seem frightening. However, focusing on safe techniques and proper form is paramount to ensure effectiveness and prevent injuries. Start with exercises that use your own body weight for resistance, such as squats, push-ups, and lunges. These exercises are foundational, helping to build your core strength and stability, which are essential for more advanced training. As you progress, incorporating free weights such as dumbbells or kettlebells can add variety and increase intensity. It's crucial to perform each exercise with the correct form to maximize benefits and minimize the risk of injury. For instance, when doing a squat, keep your feet shoulder-width apart and back straight, lowering down as if sitting in a chair, which helps protect your back and knees.

Equipment and Resources

As you delve deeper into strength training, having the right equipment can enhance your workout and help you achieve better results. Starting with the basics, resistance bands are an excellent tool, especially for beginners. They are versatile, portable, and provide varying levels of resistance that can suit any fitness level. They're particularly useful for performing exercises that target smaller muscle groups that are often neglected in traditional weight training. For those ready to advance, free weights like dumbbells and barbells allow for a wide range of exercises that can be adjusted according to your strength level. Additionally, weight machines at a gym can be particularly useful for isolating specific muscles and maintaining proper form, especially for beginners.

Using this equipment effectively requires some guidance. For beginners, it may be beneficial to consult a personal trainer who can demonstrate how to use each piece of equipment properly. Additionally, numerous online platforms offer instructional videos and detailed workout plans that can guide you through each exercise safely. When setting up a home gym, consider investing in a mix of equipment that allows for versatility in your workouts. A set of adjustable dumbbells, a resistance band set, and a stability ball can offer a comprehensive range of exercise options without requiring a large space.

Progressive Overload Principle

To continually benefit from strength training, embracing the progressive overload principle is essential. This fundamental concept involves gradually increasing the amount of resistance during your training to continue building muscle and strength. Progressive overload can be achieved by increasing the weight you lift, the number of repetitions, or the intensity of the exercises. It is crucial for ongoing improvement because muscles adapt to a given stress over time, and without increased demands, your progress will plateau.

Applying this principle might mean adding more weight to your lifts every few weeks or increasing the number of repetitions per set. Another approach is to decrease the rest intervals between sets, which can intensify the workout and lead to increased strength gains. It's important to implement these changes gradually to avoid overloading your muscles and risking injury. Keeping a detailed training log can help you track your progress and make thoughtful adjustments to your workout regimen, ensuring continuous improvement and adaptation in your strength training routine.

By incorporating these strategies into your fitness routine, strength training becomes not just a method of enhancing your physical capabilities but a vital component of a holistic approach to aging well. With each repetition, you're not just building muscle but fortifying your body against the challenges of aging, ensuring that your later years are not only longer but also stronger and more vibrant.

3.4 Cardio for Stamina: Heart Health as You Age

Understanding the pivotal role of cardiovascular exercise in maintaining heart health and overall stamina is crucial as you navigate your later years. Regular cardio workouts not only strengthen the heart muscle, making it more efficient at pumping blood throughout your body, but also help manage or prevent conditions such as high blood pressure, heart disease, and type 2 diabetes. Moreover, the benefits extend beyond physical health, impacting mental well-being by reducing stress, enhancing mood, and improving sleep quality.

Cardiovascular exercise involves any activity that increases your heart rate, breathing, and endurance. Activities suited for older adults need to consider the varying levels of fitness and mobility that can accompany aging. Brisk walking, for instance, is a highly accessible form of cardio that can be easily adjusted to fit one's fitness level. It doesn't require special equipment other than a good pair of shoes and can be done almost anywhere. The rhythmic, repetitive motion helps strengthen the heart and lungs, and being outdoors can also enhance your mental health through exposure to nature and sunlight, which boosts vitamin D levels.

Swimming is another excellent cardiovascular exercise, particularly beneficial for those with joint issues or who find other forms of exercise painful. It's a low-impact activity that provides resistance training as you move through the water, enhancing muscle strength and endurance without straining joints. Cycling, whether on a stationary bike or outdoors, is also advantageous. It increases heart rate and promotes stamina while being gentler on the hips, knees, and ankles than running. Each of these activities can be tailored to your comfort and fitness levels, allowing for gradual progression as your endurance improves.

Incorporating interval training into your cardio routine can significantly enhance its benefits, especially for heart health. Interval training alternates short bursts of intense activity with periods of lighter activity or rest. This method is highly effective at improving cardiovascular fitness and burning calories in a shorter period of time. For older adults, it's important to adapt interval training to ensure it provides a challenge without overwhelming the heart. For example, if you enjoy walking, try incorporating intervals by walking as fast as you can for one minute, then slowing down for two minutes, and repeating the cycle for 20–30 minutes. This approach helps maximize cardiovascular benefits while managing the intensity to suit your body's responses.

Monitoring Intensity

To ensure that cardiovascular exercises are done within a safe intensity range, it's critical to monitor how hard your heart is working during exercise. One simple method is the talk test. If you're able to carry on a conversation comfortably while exercising, your intensity level is likely in a good range. However, if speaking full sentences becomes difficult, you might be pushing too hard. For a more precise measurement, using a heart rate monitor can be extremely effective. These devices give you a direct look at your heart rate in real-time, allowing you to adjust your intensity to stay within target heart rate zones. These zones are typically calculated based on your age and maximum heart rate, which can be roughly estimated by subtracting your age from 220.

To integrate heart rate monitoring into your routine, start by determining your target heart rate zone, which is generally 50% to 70% of your maximum heart rate for moderate-intensity activities and 70% to 85% for vigorous activities. Wearing a heart rate monitor during your workouts can help you stay within this range, making adjustments in real-time based on the feedback you receive. For instance, if your heart rate is too low according to the monitor, you might increase your walking pace or choose a slightly more challenging route with gentle inclines. Conversely, if your heart rate spikes above the desired range, it's a cue to reduce your intensity, ensuring you're working out safely and effectively.

Embracing these practices—choosing suitable exercises, incorporating interval training, and monitoring intensity—can significantly enhance your cardiovascular health. This supports your physical stamina and enriches your quality of life, letting you enjoy more active years with reduced health risks. Whether you're starting a new exercise routine or adjusting your current activities, these strategies ensure that your cardiovascular workouts are both enjoyable and beneficial, providing a solid foundation for maintaining heart health as you age.

3.5 Low-Impact Workouts: Effective Options for Joint Preservation

Understanding the significance of low-impact workouts begins with recognizing their role in maintaining joint health and overall physical well-being. Low-impact exercises are designed to minimize the stress placed on your body, particularly your joints, making them ideal for individuals who experience joint pain, have arthritis, or are in the later stages of life where bone density and joint stability may be compromised. These workouts ensure that at least one foot remains in contact with the ground at all times, significantly reducing the impact felt through the joints compared to high-impact activities like running or jumping.

The effectiveness of low-impact exercises in preserving joint health while still providing a rigorous workout cannot be overstated. Aquatic workouts, for example, are a prime illustration of low-impact exercises. Water provides natural resistance and buoyancy, allowing you to strengthen your muscles and improve cardiovascular health without the harsh impact on your joints that similar land-based exercises might cause. This makes swimming or water aerobics excellent choices for a full-body workout that feels more like a refreshment than a chore. Another fantastic option is elliptical training, which mimics the natural path of the ankle, knee, and hip joints during walking or running, but without the substantial impact associated with these activities. The smooth, continuous motion of the elliptical helps strengthen your lower body and heart without straining your joints. Pilates, too, emphasizes controlled movements and core strength, enhancing flexibility and joint health without high-impact motions, making it suitable for all ages and fitness levels.

Incorporating these low-impact exercises into your fitness regimen requires thoughtful integration to address all aspects of physical health. Start by identifying exercises that you enjoy, and that fit your specific health needs, as this will help you maintain consistency in your routine. It's beneficial to create a balanced workout schedule that combines cardiovascular, strength, and flexibility training. For instance, you might begin your week with a water aerobics class to boost heart health, dedicate another day to Pilates to strengthen your core and improve flexibility, and use the elliptical machine mid-week to continue building stamina and muscle strength. This variety keeps your routine engaging and ensures a holistic approach to fitness that enhances multiple aspects of your health.

"Low-impact" was seen as a weakness in military culture. For people who couldn't handle "real" exercise.

I know differently now. Low-impact isn't weakness—it's wisdom.

High-impact (20s-40s):

- Running on concrete in combat boots
- Overhead lifts with improper form
- Heavy load-bearing without recovery

Low-impact (rebuilding at 58):

- Water aerobics
- Elliptical
- Pilates
- Walking

High-impact destroyed my joints. Low-impact is preserving what's left.

But here's the dependence: I don't get to choose anymore. My body decided for me. I'm dependent on low-impact because I destroyed my capacity for anything else.

If you still have a choice—if your joints work, shoulders function—choose wisely. Choose sustainable over impressive. Choose exercises you can do at 70, not ones that leave you dependent Balancing the impact and intensity of your workouts is vital to gaining the benefits of exercise while protecting your joints. Start at a moderate pace that challenges you without causing discomfort, and gradually increase the intensity as your fitness improves. Pay attention to your body's signals. Discomfort or pain during or after a workout is a clear indicator that you need to adjust the intensity or switch to a gentler activity. Using equipment like cushioned mats during Pilates, wearing supportive footwear while using the elliptical, or choosing a heated pool for aquatic exercises can further reduce the risk of joint pain and enhance your comfort during workouts.

Embracing low-impact workouts as part of your exercise regimen is more than a fitness choice; it's a commitment to preserving your body's mobility and quality of life. By carefully selecting activities that bolster your health without overburdening your joints, you create a sustainable fitness plan that supports your well-being at every age. This approach keeps you active and independent and enriches your life, allowing you to engage more fully with the world around you.

As this chapter concludes, we reflect on the essential strategies and benefits of incorporating physical wellness and exercise into your lifestyle, particularly as you age. From tailoring your fitness regime to integrating low-impact workouts, each step contributes to a healthier, more vibrant version of yourself. These practices are not just about maintaining physical health; they are about creating a lifestyle that supports longevity and enhances your quality of life.

Physical wellness strategies work—but only if you apply them before destroying your body.

Only if you customize to YOUR body, not external ideals.

Only if you treat pain as information, not weakness.

Only if you value sustainable capability over impressive performance.

I learned this too late. These days, I'm rebuilding within permanent limitations, managing chronic pain, and accepting dependence.

You don't have to learn this way. You can choose differently. Build sustainable strength NOW while you have choices.

You can age into your 60s, 70s, 80s with independence intact—carrying luggage, opening jars, lifting grandchildren, doing what matters without constant help.

I don't have that anymore. But you can.

Don't wait until your body chooses for you.

Looking ahead, the next chapter will explore the interplay between mental wellness and your physical health, underscoring the importance of nurturing both to achieve a harmonious balance. As you continue to build on the foundations laid in this chapter, remember that each step forward is a step towards a more fulfilling and active life.

Chapter 4: Cognitive Health and Mental Acuity

I'm terrified my brain is going the way of my shoulder.

That's the fear I live with now: that after spending decades destroying my body, my mind will be next. Or maybe it's already happening, and I can't see it clearly enough to know.

Bipolar disorder already affects my cognition. The medications I take to manage it have cognitive side effects—slower processing speed, word-finding difficulties, and memory gaps. The manic episodes create periods where my thinking is distorted, my judgment impaired, my perception of reality altered. The depressive episodes create brain fog so thick I can barely string thoughts together.

Layer chronic pain on top of that—pain that disrupts sleep, which disrupts cognitive function. Pain medications that further cloud thinking. The constant low-grade stress of living in a body that hurts, which elevates cortisol, which damages the hippocampus, which affects memory formation.

Then add the sleep disruption from both bipolar disorder and chronic pain. Decades of inadequate sleep. Decades of my brain not getting the restorative rest it needs to clear out metabolic waste, consolidate memories, regulate mood, and repair cellular damage.

And now I'm 58, watching for signs:

- Did I forget that word because I'm tired, or because my brain is declining?

- Am I having trouble following this conversation because it's complex, or because my processing speed is slowing?

- Did I lose my train of thought because I was distracted, or because my working memory is failing?

- Am I making this mistake because I'm stressed, or because my executive function is compromised?

I can't always tell the difference. And that uncertainty is terrifying.

My mind is my livelihood now. I can't work outside the home because my body failed. Writing is what I have left. Learning is what keeps me engaged. My cognitive capacity is, literally, all I have left to offer the world.

What happens when that goes too far?

This chapter covers brain games, stress management, meditation, and mental fitness routines—all evidence-based strategies for maintaining cognitive health. That information is solid and important.

But I'm also going to tell you what it's like to live with the fear of cognitive decline when you already have conditions that affect cognition. When you can't separate "normal aging" from "medication side effects" from "bipolar symptoms" from "sleep deprivation" from "actual decline."

When every forgotten word feels like a harbinger of dementia. When every moment of confusion feels like proof that your brain is failing.

This is the fear that keeps me awake at night (which ironically makes the cognitive issues worse, creating a vicious cycle I can't escape).

Let me show you both: the science of maintaining cognitive health AND the reality of living with cognitive fear.

4.1 Brain Games That Actually Work

Efficacy of Brain Games

The notion that brain games can function as cognitive enhancers is more than just wishful thinking; it's a hypothesis that has been rigorously tested and supported by scientific research. Studies have shown that engaging in specific types of brain games can lead to noticeable improvements in various cognitive domains, such as memory, attention, processing speed, and problem-solving skills. For instance, a study published in the journal "Neuropsychology" demonstrated that participants who regularly engaged in puzzle-based games showed improvements in tasks requiring cognitive flexibility, attention, and memory. These games stimulate the brain by presenting challenges that require the player to think critically, strategize, and make rapid decisions, thereby potentially increasing neural activity and promoting the development of new neural pathways.

I use brain games religiously. Not because I enjoy them particularly, but because I'm desperately trying to maintain cognitive function despite everything working against me.

Why I started:

After my shoulder surgery, after I couldn't work anymore, after bipolar medication changes affected my cognition, I needed something I could DO. Some way to actively fight back against cognitive decline instead of just watching it happen.

Brain games gave me that sense of control. Lumosity, Peak, crossword puzzles, Sudoku—I do them all. I track my performance obsessively, looking for patterns, watching for decline.

What I've noticed:

On good days (stable mood, decent sleep, low pain), my scores are higher. I'm faster, more accurate, and better at problem-solving.

On bad days (manic or depressive episode, poor sleep, high pain), my scores plummet. I can barely complete tasks that felt easy yesterday.

What this teaches me:

My cognitive performance isn't fixed—it's variable, dependent on multiple factors I can only partially control. The brain games don't "fix" anything, but they give me data. They show me what helps (sleep, stable mood, pain management) and what hurts (stress, medication changes, poor nutrition).

The obsessive piece:

I have to be careful not to let brain games become another way to punish myself. Another metric by which I'm "failing." Another thing I'm not doing "well enough."

Some days I have to remind myself: Lower scores aren't moral failures. They're data points showing my brain needs support, not criticism.

What I wish I'd known in my 30s:

Cognitive health requires the same attention as physical health. That sleep matters for brain function as much as for muscle recovery. That chronic stress literally shrinks your hippocampus. That you can't "push through" cognitive exhaustion the way I tried to push through physical exhaustion.

If I'd protected my sleep, managed my stress, stabilized my bipolar disorder earlier, and addressed my pain earlier—my cognitive baseline might be higher now. My reserves might be deeper.

But I didn't. I treated my brain like I treated my body: as something to be pushed until it broke.

Now I'm doing brain games, trying to maintain what I have left, terrified of losing more.

Recommended Games

Navigating through the plethora of available brain games can be daunting; however, some have been consistently recommended for their proven benefits. 'Lumosity', a well-crafted app consisting of games that target attention, memory, flexibility, speed of processing, and problem-solving skills, stands out for its scientific foundation and adaptability to your performance levels. Another notable mention is 'Peak,' which offers over 40 games designed to challenge your cognitive abilities and track your progress. Each game on 'Peak' focuses on specific skills such as mental agility, language, coordination, and emotion control, providing a comprehensive brain workout. Additionally, 'CogniFit' offers games that assess and train a wide array of cognitive abilities and provide detailed feedback on your performance, allowing you to monitor your progress and identify areas needing improvement. And for those of us who have a love-hate relationship with technology or just prefer old-fashioned pen and paper, we shouldn't discount crosswords, word searches, Sudoku, and other mind stretchers available in a wide range of formats in books and magazines.

Regular Practice

To reap the cognitive benefits of brain games, consistency is key. Just as physical exercise requires regularity to improve fitness, cognitive exercises need to be engaged with routinely to enhance brain function. Establishing a routine for brain training can help incorporate this practice into your daily life seamlessly. For effective results, it is recommended to spend about 15 minutes, three to four times a week, playing brain games. Fifteen minutes, three to four times a week. That's the recommendation.

I do more. Much more. Because I'm not just trying to "enhance" my cognition—I'm trying to PRESERVE it against multiple threats.

My actual practice:

- Brain games: 30-45 minutes daily

- Crossword puzzles: Every morning with coffee (you don't have to finish the whole thing in the15 minutes it takes to finish your coffee)

- Reading: At least an hour daily (often more when writing)

- Writing: Multiple hours most days

- Learning: Previously learned programming

This isn't "recommended practice." This is **cognitive panic.**

The compulsive piece:

I have to be careful. There's a difference between "engaging in cognitive activities because they're enjoyable and beneficial" and "engaging in cognitive activities because I'm terrified that if I stop, my brain will deteriorate."

I'm working on finding the balance. Most days I fail.

What bipolar disorder adds to this:

During manic episodes, I can do brain games for HOURS without feeling fatigued. My scores skyrocket. I feel brilliant, invincible, like I'm "solving" cognitive decline through sheer willpower.

During depressive episodes, I can barely complete one game. My scores drop. I feel stupid, broken, like my brain is already gone.

Neither extreme is accurate. Both feel absolutely real in the moment.

The lesson I'm slowly learning:

Consistency matters more than intensity. Regular, moderate practice beats manic binge sessions followed by depressive crashes. But "consistency" is hard when your mood, energy, and cognitive capacity fluctuate wildly.

I'm still figuring this out. After decades of punishing my body, now I'm trying not to punish my brain in the same way.

This schedule is manageable for most people and sufficient to stimulate cognitive improvements over time. It's also important to vary the types of games you play to ensure all cognitive domains are being challenged, which can prevent plateaus in mental fitness.

Combining Games with Other Activities

While brain games are powerful tools for cognitive enhancement, they are most effective when used in conjunction with other brain-enriching activities. Reading, for instance, not only improves vocabulary and comprehension but also enhances connectivity in the brain. Puzzle-solving, such as crosswords or Sudoku, requires logic and pattern recognition, skills that are also honed by many brain games. Engaging in discussions or debates on challenging topics can further sharpen your reasoning and verbal communication skills. Integrating these activities with regular brain game practice creates a robust cognitive exercise regimen that prevents cognitive decline and fosters an intellectually stimulating lifestyle.

Exploring this multifaceted approach to cognitive enhancement ensures that your mental acuity is not just maintained but continually revitalized, empowering you to face life's challenges with confidence and agility. As you integrate these practices into your daily routine, remember that each puzzle solved, each problem tackled, and each new concept mastered is a step toward a sharper, more vibrant mind.

4.2 Mental Health: Combating Midlife Stress and Anxiety

In the thick of midlife, you may find yourself juggling more responsibilities than ever before. The pressures of advancing in your career, managing family dynamics, and addressing evolving health concerns can often converge, creating a perfect storm of stress and anxiety. Recognizing and addressing these stressors proactively can help you maintain not only your mental health but also your overall quality of life during these pivotal years.

The first step in managing stress effectively is to identify its primary sources. Career pressures at this stage might include high expectations for performance, leadership roles, or the challenge of balancing professional growth with personal life. Family responsibilities could involve caring for aging parents while supporting your own children, often referred to as the "sandwich generation" challenges. Health concerns may also become more prominent as signs of aging or chronic conditions begin to manifest, necessitating more attention and care. Acknowledging these stressors is crucial as it forms the basis for addressing them. It's important to note that stress is not an indicator of a life poorly managed but rather a common response to the substantial responsibilities that come with midlife.

Once stressors are identified, employing effective stress management techniques can greatly alleviate their impact. Time management strategies are particularly beneficial. These might include setting realistic goals, prioritizing tasks, and perhaps most importantly, learning to say no when necessary. This can help prevent overcommitment, a common source of stress. Implementing a robust system for managing time can also foster a sense of control, significantly reducing feelings of being overwhelmed. Another effective technique is the practice of mindfulness, which involves staying present and fully engaging with the current moment. This practice can reduce the tendency to worry about future tasks or dwell on past events, both common in midlife as you reflect on your achievements and plan for the future.

My stress sources at 58:

Career pressure: Gone. I can't work. That sounds like it should reduce stress, right? Wrong. The stress of NOT being able to work, of watching my earning potential disappear, of feeling useless and irrelevant—that's worse than work stress ever was.

Family responsibilities: Caring for aging parents (like many in the "sandwich generation"), supporting adult children, maintaining relationships with my husband despite chronic pain and bipolar episodes that make me difficult to live with.

Health concerns: Chronic pain, permanent shoulder disability, bipolar disorder, sleep disorders, medication management, nutritional deficiencies from decades of disordered eating, fear of cognitive decline, fear of becoming more dependent, fear of ending up indigent and homeless.

Financial stress: Unable to work, living on disability income, terrified of running out of money, knowing I can't increase my income because my body won't cooperate, watching inflation erode what little security I have.

Identity crisis: Who am I if I can't work? What's my purpose if my body is broken? What's my value if I'm dependent on others? What happens when my mind goes too?

This isn't "midlife stress." This is a midlife crisis compounded by disability, mental illness, chronic pain, and the consequences of decades spent destroying my body.

The cognitive impact of chronic stress:

All this stress elevates cortisol. Chronically elevated cortisol damages the hippocampus (memory center), shrinks the prefrontal cortex (executive function), and enlarges the amygdala (fear center). Literally. Measurably. On brain scans.

Every day I spend in high stress is a day I'm damaging my brain. Creating the very cognitive decline I'm terrified of. The fear of decline creates stress that accelerates decline. It's a vicious cycle I can't break.

What makes this harder with bipolar disorder:

Stress triggers bipolar episodes. Episodes create more stress. The medication I take to prevent episodes has cognitive side effects. So I'm choosing between: (a) unmedicated and cognitively sharper but at risk of devastating manic/depressive episodes, or (b) medicated and cognitively slower but more stable.

There's no good choice. Just trade-offs.

In some cases, professional help may be necessary to manage stress and anxiety effectively. Mental health professionals specializing in adult psychology can offer support and therapies tailored to your specific needs. Cognitive-behavioral therapy (CBT), for example, is a treatment that has been proven effective in managing anxiety and stress by changing negative patterns of thought and behavior. Seeking such help is a sign of strength and a proactive step towards maintaining your mental health. To find a qualified professional, consider resources such as the American Psychological Association's psychologist locator or seek recommendations from your primary care physician, who can refer you to a specialist.

Creating a supportive environment is equally crucial in combating stress and promoting mental well-being. At home, this might mean establishing boundaries that help you balance family time with personal time, ensuring that you have space to relax and recharge. It's also beneficial to foster open communication with family members about each person's needs and how you can support each other. At work, try to cultivate a network of support among colleagues who understand the pressures of your role. This can involve more practical arrangements like sharing responsibilities or emotional support like having someone to talk to about work challenges.

Incorporating these strategies into your daily life can transform your midlife experience, turning what might seem like an overwhelming phase into a period of growth and fulfillment. By managing stress effectively, you not only enhance your own well-being but also set a positive example for those around you, demonstrating that midlife can be a vibrant and productive stage of life.

Stress management techniques I actually use:

Time management: Doesn't work when bipolar disorder makes your energy and capability unpredictable. I can't "prioritize tasks" when I don't know if tomorrow I'll be manic (capable of everything) or depressive (capable of nothing).

Mindfulness: This one actually helps. When I can do it. When I'm not too manic (mind racing too fast) or too depressive (mind too foggy). On stable days, mindfulness reduces stress measurably. On unstable days, it's impossible.

Professional help: I have a psychiatrist for medication management and a therapist for cognitive-behavioral work. Both are essential. Neither can "fix" the underlying reality: I'm disabled, in pain, financially insecure, and terrified of further decline.

What actually reduces my stress most:

- Writing (processes the fear, makes meaning from suffering)

- Art journaling (when words fail)

- Pilates (gentle physical engagement that doesn't hurt)

- My husband (who hasn't left despite everything)

- Small accomplishments (finishing a chapter, learning something new)

But none of these SOLVE the problems creating the stress. They just help me cope with problems that won't go away.

The cognitive health piece:

Managing stress isn't optional if I want to preserve cognitive function. It's essential. But managing stress when your life circumstances are objectively stressful isn't a matter of "techniques"—it's a matter of radical acceptance of what can't be changed, combined with aggressive intervention in what can.

I can't change my disability. I can change my response to it.

I can't change my bipolar disorder. I can manage it more effectively.

I can't change my chronic pain. I can reduce activities that make it worse.

I can't change my financial reality. I can reduce spending and stop catastrophizing about becoming homeless.

This is the work. Daily. Exhausting. Essential.

Because chronic stress is destroying my brain, and I can't afford to lose what's left.

4.3 The Importance of Sleep in Cognitive Maintenance

Understanding the profound impact of sleep on cognitive functions provides a clearer picture of its role in our daily lives, especially as we age. Adequate sleep is not merely a restorative break for the body; it's a critical period during which the brain processes and consolidates memories, refines the skills learned during the day, and clears out toxins that could potentially impair long-term cognitive functions. During the deep stages of sleep, particularly the rapid eye movement (REM) phase, the brain actively consolidates information and memories from the day. This process is vital for memory retention, helping you remember and process new information more effectively. Furthermore, sufficient sleep supports neural plasticity, the brain's ability to adapt to new information and experiences, which is essential for learning and problem-solving.

Establishing good sleep hygiene practices is crucial for maintaining cognitive health and ensuring the quality of sleep needed to support these brain functions. Setting a regular sleep schedule by going to bed and waking up at the same time every day helps regulate your body's internal clock, or circadian rhythm, which can improve the quality of your sleep. Creating an optimal sleep environment is also key. This means making your bedroom conducive to sleep—cool, quiet, and dark. Investing in a comfortable mattress and pillows can significantly improve sleep quality, as physical discomfort is a common barrier to a good night's sleep. Additionally, developing a pre-sleep routine that promotes relaxation can be very beneficial. This might include activities such as reading a book, taking a warm bath, or practicing relaxation exercises like deep breathing or progressive muscle relaxation. These activities signal to your body that it's time to wind down and transition into sleep, making it easier to fall asleep and stay asleep throughout the night.

Sleep is where everything falls apart for me.

The bipolar disorder piece:

Manic episodes destroy sleep. I go days with 2-3 hours per night, feeling completely functional, convinced I don't need more. Then I crash.

Depressive episodes disrupt sleep differently—either sleeping 12+ hours and waking exhausted, or insomnia from rumination and despair.

Even on stable days, bipolar disorder affects sleep architecture. My brain doesn't cycle through sleep stages normally. I don't get adequate deep sleep or REM sleep even when I'm in bed for 8 hours.

The chronic pain piece:

Pain wakes me up. Multiple times per night. Every position hurts my shoulder. Rolling over triggers pain. Reaching for the pillow creates pain.

Pain medications help but create their own sleep disruption— some make me groggy but don't actually improve sleep quality; others wear off halfway through the night.

The cognitive impact:

I KNOW sleep deprivation affects cognition. I know the research. During sleep, your brain clears out metabolic waste products (including beta-amyloid proteins that contribute to Alzheimer's). It consolidates memories. It repairs cellular damage. It regulates mood and hormones.

When you don't get adequate sleep—especially adequate deep sleep and REM sleep—all of those processes are compromised.

My sleep reality:

I average 5-6 hours per night. Rarely 7. Almost never 8. by 0800 often interrupted multiple times. Frequently poor quality even when I'm asleep.

I've been sleep-deprived for DECADES. First from military schedules and deployments. Then from shift work. Then from chronic pain. Now from the combination of pain, bipolar disorder, and aging.

What this means for cognitive health:

Every night of poor sleep is a night my brain isn't clearing out waste products. Isn't consolidating memories properly. Isn't repairing damage. Isn't regulating hormones effectively.

Decades of this has consequences I can't see directly but know must exist. Accumulated damage. Increased risk of cognitive decline. Faster aging of my brain.

What I'm doing about it:

- Sleep hygiene (dark room, cool temperature, consistent bedtime)
- Medication management (working with psychiatrist to optimize)
- Pain management (heating pad, positioning, medication timing)
- Acceptance that I'll never be a "good sleeper"

- -Start using CPAP to relieve/correct Sleep Apnea

But I can't fix the underlying problems. I can only manage them. And some nights, even management fails.

The fear:

That decades of inadequate sleep have already done irreversible damage to my cognitive health. That I'm starting from a deficit I can't overcome. That every intervention now is "too little, too late."

I don't know if this fear is rational. But it's real. And it keeps me awake at night. Which makes the sleep problem worse. Another vicious cycle.

Dealing with sleep disorders becomes increasingly important as we age, as conditions like insomnia and sleep apnea tend to become more prevalent. Insomnia, characterized by difficulty falling or staying asleep, can severely impact your daily functioning and cognitive health if not addressed. Sleep apnea, a condition where breathing repeatedly stops and starts during sleep, can lead to fragmented sleep and reduced oxygen levels in the blood, which may impair cognitive functions over time. If you experience symptoms of these or other sleep disorders, such as excessive daytime sleepiness, loud snoring, or noticeable pauses in breathing during sleep, it's important to seek medical advice. A healthcare provider can assess your symptoms and may recommend a sleep study to diagnose the issue accurately. Treatment options vary depending on the diagnosis but could include lifestyle changes, medical devices to aid breathing during sleep, or in some cases, surgery.

In addition to these practices, incorporating natural sleep aids and lifestyle changes can further enhance sleep quality. Dietary adjustments play a significant role; for instance, limiting caffeine and alcohol intake, especially in the hours leading up to bedtime, can prevent disruptions to your sleep cycle. Eating a light evening meal, particularly one that includes foods rich in tryptophan, magnesium, and calcium, can promote better sleep. These nutrients aid in the production of melatonin, the hormone that regulates sleep-wake cycles, and provide muscle relaxation. By the way, turkey is a good source of this amino acid, but you'd have to eat 20 servings of turkey to equal the required daily dose. Instead, you can try cheese, chicken, fish, milk, peanuts, egg whites, and soybeans. Also, sunflower, pumpkin and sesame seeds. Engaging in regular physical activity is another effective method for improving sleep. Exercise not only helps to expend energy and reduce stress, which can make it easier to fall asleep, but it also promotes deeper, more restorative sleep. However, it's important to avoid vigorous exercise close to bedtime, as it can have the opposite effect and keep you awake.

Through a combination of good sleep hygiene, addressing sleep disorders, and natural sleep aids, you can significantly enhance your sleep quality. This, in turn, supports your cognitive functions—crucial for maintaining mental clarity, memory, and problem-solving abilities—as you navigate the complexities of aging. Remember, sleep is not just a passive state; it's an active period of mental and physical restoration that plays a critical role in how well you think, learn, and function throughout your life.

4.4 Meditation Techniques for a Sharper Mind

Meditation, once viewed as an esoteric practice, has now gained widespread recognition for its profound benefits on mental clarity and emotional stability. Its appeal lies not just in its simplicity but also in its versatility, offering a range of techniques that cater to different preferences and objectives. Among these, mindfulness, focused attention, and loving-kindness meditations are particularly noteworthy for their positive effects on cognitive health. Mindfulness meditation encourages you to observe your present experiences, thoughts, and feelings without judgment, enhancing your awareness and acceptance. This practice can lead to improved focus and reduced stress, as it trains you to remain calm and attentive despite external distractions. Focused attention meditation, on the other hand, involves concentrating on a single point of reference—be it your breath, a mantra, or a specific object. This technique strengthens your ability to concentrate, improving your attention span and helping you control the whirlwind of thoughts that often invade your mind. Loving-kindness meditation, or meta meditation, focuses on developing feelings of compassion and love, first towards oneself and then radiating outward. This form of meditation can significantly enhance your emotional resilience, reducing feelings of isolation and boosting overall well-being.

The scientific community has backed these practices with substantial research demonstrating their benefits. Studies have shown that regular meditation can lead to structural changes in the brain, particularly in areas associated with memory, self-awareness, empathy, and stress. For instance, research published in "Psychiatry Research: Neuroimaging" has shown that mindfulness meditation can lead to increased gray matter density in the hippocampus, known for its role in learning and memory and in structures associated with self-awareness, compassion, and introspection. Another study highlighted in "The Journal of Psychological Science" found that just a few weeks of training in mindfulness meditation significantly improved focus and cognitive flexibility. These findings underscore meditation's role in enhancing mental capacities that are crucial for navigating the complexities of modern life.

For those new to meditation, the digital age offers an abundance of resources that make learning and practicing meditation more accessible than ever. Apps like 'Headspace' and 'Calm' provide guided meditation sessions that can be easily integrated into your daily routine. These platforms offer a variety of guided sessions, from brief meditations for busy days to longer sessions aimed at deepening your practice. They also feature a range of focuses, including anxiety reduction, sleep improvement, and pain management. Local classes, often available at yoga studios or community centers, provide the added benefit of learning from experienced instructors who can offer personalized guidance and feedback. These classes also offer the opportunity to meditate in a group setting, which can enhance your practice through the shared energy and focus of multiple participants.

Incorporating meditation into your daily life can be as simple as dedicating a few minutes each morning or evening to practice. Creating a designated meditation space in your home can enhance this routine, making it a special part of your day that you look forward to. This space doesn't need to be elaborate—a comfortable chair or cushion in a quiet corner is sufficient. The key is consistency; even short daily sessions can yield noticeable benefits over time. For those with hectic schedules, integrating mindfulness practices into daily activities such as eating or walking can be effective. Mindful eating involves paying full attention to the experience of eating, savoring each bite, and acknowledging your body's hunger and fullness signals, which can improve your relationship with food. Similarly, mindful walking involves focusing entirely on the experience of walking, noticing the sensation of your feet touching the ground, the rhythm of your breath, and the sights and sounds around you. This practice can transform a simple daily activity into a rich, restorative experience.

By embracing these meditation techniques and integrating them into your lifestyle, you enhance cognitive function and improve emotional health, paving the way for a more focused, resilient, and balanced life. Whether you are seeking to reduce stress, improve concentration, or cultivate a greater sense of inner peace, meditation offers a powerful tool that adjusts to meet your personal goals and lifestyle, enriching your journey toward optimal mental health.

Meditation is one of the few interventions that helps with ALL my problems: reduces stress, improves sleep (when I can fall asleep), manages pain (changes my relationship to it if not the pain itself), stabilizes mood, and potentially protects cognitive function.

Why it's hard with bipolar disorder:

During mania: My mind races too fast to meditate. Sitting still feels impossible. "Observing thoughts" is futile when I have thousands per minute. Traditional meditation instructions don't work when your brain is in overdrive.

During depression: Meditation can become rumination. "Observing thoughts" means watching an endless loop of negative, self-critical, despairing thoughts. Sometimes this makes things worse, not better.

On stable days: Meditation works beautifully. Reduces stress. Improves focus. Creates mental clarity. I can actually DO what the instructions describe.

What I've learned:

I need different meditation approaches for different mood states.

For mania: Movement meditation (walking meditation), very short sessions (5 minutes max), focus on physical sensations rather than thoughts.

For depression: Guided meditations with positive focus, compassion practices, very gentle self-talk, permission to stop if it's making things worse.

For stable periods: Traditional mindfulness practice, body scans, breath focus, 15-20 minute sessions.

The cognitive benefits:

When I can meditate regularly (during stable periods), I notice:

- Better focus and concentration

- Improved working memory

- Faster processing when switching between tasks

- Reduced anxiety about cognitive decline (ironically, worrying less about it helps)

- Better emotional regulation (which reduces stress, which protects cognition)

What I wish I'd started earlier:

If I'd developed a meditation practice in my 30s, I might have:
- Recognized bipolar episodes earlier (more self-awareness)
- Managed stress better (less cortisol damage to the brain)
- Slept better (meditation improves sleep quality)
- Reduced chronic pain impact (changes pain perception)
- Protected cognitive function proactively instead of reactively

But I didn't. Because meditation looked like "doing nothing" and I was trained to always be "doing something." Because stillness felt like weakness. Because I didn't understand that training your mind is as important as training your body.

Now I meditate. Not as often as I should. Not as consistently as would be ideal. But when I do, it helps.

And every session feels like a small victory against the cognitive decline I'm terrified of.

4.5 Building a Routine for Mental Fitness

Creating a daily routine that prioritizes mental fitness is akin to building a scaffold that supports the architecture of your cognitive health. Just as a varied diet nourishes the body, a diverse regimen of activities can enrich your mind. Engaging in reading, writing, and stimulating conversations each day can significantly enhance cognitive function. These activities challenge the brain, keeping it active and engaged. For instance, reading exposes you to new ideas and perspectives, enhancing cognitive flexibility. Writing, from journaling to creative compositions, improves language skills and can be a powerful tool for processing and reflecting on your experiences. Stimulating conversations, whether debating a recent news article or sharing insights from a book, encourages you to think critically and articulate your thoughts clearly, sharpening your mental acuity.

My actual mental fitness routine:

Reading: 1-2 hours daily (when depression allows, more when manic)
- Fiction for pleasure and empathy
- Non-fiction for learning
- Research for my writing projects

Writing: 2-4 hours most days

- Books (like this one)
- Articles and blog posts
- Journal entries for processing emotions
- Creative writing for joy

Stimulating conversations:

- With my husband (when I'm stable enough for real dialogue)
- With other writers and creatives (online communities)
- Limited due to disability and isolation

Physical exercise is often touted for its benefits to bodily health, but its impact on the brain is equally profound. Aerobic exercises, such as jogging, cycling, or swimming, increase the heart rate, which pumps more oxygen to the brain and aids the release of hormones that provide an excellent environment for the growth of brain cells. Exercise also promotes neuroplasticity by stimulating the production of growth factors, which are involved in creating new neural connections. The dual benefits for both physical and cognitive health make regular physical activity a cornerstone of a holistic approach to mental fitness. Incorporating at least 30 minutes of moderate-intensity exercise into your daily routine can help maintain both brain function and overall health.

The rest of my mental fitness routine:

Brain games: 30-45 minutes daily

- Lumosity, Peak, crosswords, Sudoku

- Obsessive tracking of performance

- Sometimes helpful, sometimes anxiety-inducing

Learning new skills:

- Currently German language

- Previously: programming, web development

- Constantly seeking new challenges

This looks impressive written out. Like, I'm doing everything right for cognitive health.

What it doesn't show:

The variability: On depressive days, I might read for 20 minutes and that's all I can manage. On manic days, I might do ALL of these things for 16 hours straight and feel brilliant. On painful days, I can't concentrate on anything complex.

The fear driving it: I'm not doing this because I love it (though I often do). I'm doing it because I'm terrified that if I stop, my brain will deteriorate faster. This isn't healthy motivation—it's panic masked as productivity.

The physical limitations: I can't exercise like I used to. Can't do "30 minutes of moderate-intensity" anything because my shoulder won't tolerate it. So I'm leaning HARD on cognitive activities because physical activities are limited.

The isolation factor: "Stimulating conversations" are harder when you're disabled, don't work, can't easily leave the house, and have bipolar disorder that makes you difficult to be around sometimes.

Nutrition also plays a critical role in cognitive health. The brain requires a constant supply of fuel. This fuel comes from the foods you eat, and the quality of that fuel can significantly affect how well your brain functions. Foods rich in omega-3 fatty acids, such as salmon and walnuts, are known to enhance the structural integrity of brain cells. Blueberries, often termed 'brain berries,' are packed with antioxidants that reduce oxidative stress and inflammation, pathways that can contribute to brain aging and neurodegenerative diseases. Dark chocolate, rich in flavonoids, caffeine, and antioxidants, boosts mood and improves memory and slows down cognitive decline. Incorporating these foods into your diet can support brain health and enhance cognitive functions such as memory, concentration, and processing speed.

What I'm actually eating now for cognitive health:

Omega-3 fatty acids: Fish 2-3 times per week, walnuts, flaxseed. This one, I can actually do consistently because I finally learned (at 58) that fat isn't the enemy.

Antioxidants: Berries every morning (in yogurt or smoothies), dark chocolate (medicinal, obviously), leafy greens. Easier to maintain now that I'm not doing "salad week" crash diets.

Brain-supporting nutrients: B-vitamins (supplement because decades of restriction created deficiencies), vitamin D (supplement because I don't go outside enough), magnesium (helps with sleep and cognition both).

What I can't do perfectly:

Eliminate sugar (I use it for emotional regulation sometimes, which isn't ideal but is reality). Eat "clean" all the time (some days, getting any food into my body is success). Meal prep like the books recommend (energy levels too variable).

The cognitive impact of my past eating patterns:

All those years of crash dieting, "salad week," restricting calories—that created nutritional deficiencies that affected my brain. Iron deficiency affects concentration. B-vitamin deficiency affects mood and cognition. Inadequate healthy fats affect brain structure and hormone production.

I'm trying to repair decades of damage with better nutrition now. But some damage may be permanent.

Regular assessments of your cognitive health are vital to maintaining mental fitness. They help you gauge the effectiveness of your routine and make necessary adjustments. Various online tools and apps can track cognitive performance through games and tasks designed to measure areas like memory, attention, and problem-solving skills. Regular check-ins with these tools can help you identify areas where you might need to increase your mental fitness efforts. These assessments can be as simple as reflecting on your ability to recall information, solve complex problems, or learn new skills. Keeping a log of your performance can provide insights into your cognitive health over time, helping you stay committed to your mental fitness goals.

This approach to building a routine for mental fitness encapsulates activities that maintain and enhance your cognitive capabilities. By nurturing your brain with a mix of intellectual stimulation, physical activity, proper nutrition, and regular assessments, you are not just preserving your mental faculties but actively enriching them. This routine supports your cognitive health and enhances your overall quality of life, helping your mind remain as vibrant and agile as possible.

As we close this chapter on mental fitness, remember that each component of your daily routine contributes to a larger picture of cognitive health. From the foods you eat to the exercises you perform and the intellectual activities you engage in, each element plays a key role in maintaining and enhancing your mental acuity. Looking forward, the next chapter will explore emotional well-being and social connections, further expanding on how to maintain a balanced and fulfilling lifestyle as you age.

Chapter 5: Emotional Well-Being and Social Connections

When you can't work, you become invisible.

That's what I've learned at this "ripe old age', unable to hold a job outside the home, disabled by a shoulder I destroyed proving I wasn't "excess baggage," managing bipolar disorder that makes me difficult to be around, living in chronic pain that limits where I can go and what I can do.

Society sees you differently when you're not productive. When you're not contributing economically. When you're not "doing something" that fits their definition of valuable.

I'm invisible in multiple, intersecting ways:

As a disabled woman: Society already dismisses women over 50. Add disability, and you disappear entirely. People look through you, not at you. Conversations happen around you, not with you.

As someone who can't work: In a culture that defines worth by productivity, inability to work equals worthlessness. "What do you do?" is the first question at any social gathering. "I'm disabled and can't work" ends conversations fast.

As someone with mental illness: Bipolar disorder carries stigma. People get uncomfortable. Worried you'll be "unstable" or "dramatic" or "too much." It's easier to just... not invite you. Not include you. Not see you.

As someone in chronic pain: Pain is invisible to others but omnipresent to you. You can't do spontaneous activities. Can't commit to events because you don't know if you'll be in too much pain. People stop asking after you cancel enough times.

The intersection of all of these: Woman + over 50 + disabled + mentally ill + in chronic pain + can't work = invisible. Irrelevant. Easy to forget. Easier not to see at all.

This chapter is about emotional well-being and social connections—maintaining relationships, avoiding isolation, finding purpose, managing grief, and cultivating joy.

All are crucial for healthy aging. All evidence-based. All important.

But here's what the research doesn't always acknowledge: some isolation isn't about "poor social skills" or "not trying hard enough." Some isolation is structural. Systemic. The predictable result of being someone society would rather not see.

I'm going to share the science of emotional well-being and social connection. But I'm also going to tell you what it's like to be invisible. To watch yourself become irrelevant. To fight against isolation while living in a body and with conditions that make connection extraordinarily difficult.

Because you can't fix isolation by "just joining a book club" when the problem isn't your effort—it's that society has decided you don't matter.

Let me show you both: the strategies that work AND the reality that complicates them.

5.1 Avoiding Isolation: Building and Maintaining Social Connections

Recognizing Signs of Isolation

Isolation creeps in silently, often masked by the hustle of daily routines. Recognizing its signs is the first step in combating its subtle onset. You might feel persistent loneliness, a sense of being disconnected even in a crowd, or find yourself withdrawing from social interactions you once enjoyed. These feelings can be accompanied by physical symptoms such as sleep disturbances, changes in appetite, or reduced energy levels. The impact of prolonged isolation isn't merely discomforting; it's detrimental and linked to increased risks of severe medical conditions, including heart disease, depression, and cognitive decline. The correlation between social isolation and accelerated cognitive decline, in particular, is supported by numerous studies, suggesting that human interaction plays a more significant role in our mental health than previously understood.

My signs of isolation:

Persistent loneliness: Check. Even when my husband is home, even when I'm talking to people online, there's a fundamental loneliness that comes from being invisible to the world outside my house.

Disconnected even in a crowd: I can't test this much anymore because I'm rarely in crowds. Chronic pain and disability limit my ability to go places. But when I do go out—doctor's appointments, rare social events—yes, absolutely disconnected. People talk around me, not to me.

Withdrawing from social interactions: This one's complicated. Am I withdrawing, or am I being excluded? Am I choosing isolation, or is it being imposed on me by physical limitations, pain, bipolar episodes, or financial constraints?

Physical symptoms: Sleep disturbances (yes, but also from pain and bipolar). Change in appetite (yes, but also from depression and medication). Decline in energy (yes, but also from chronic pain and disability).

The vicious cycle:

- Isolation → depression → less energy to reach out → more isolation
- Pain → can't attend events → people stop inviting you → more isolation
- Bipolar episodes → act "difficult" → people withdraw → more isolation
- Can't work → lose work friends → no daily social contact → more isolation

What the research says: "Social isolation is linked to increased risks of serious medical conditions, including heart disease, depression, and cognitive decline."

What I know: I'm living all of those risks. The isolation isn't just uncomfortable—it's literally dangerous to my health. But knowing that doesn't make it easier to fix.

The invisibility piece:

When you become invisible, people don't intentionally exclude you. They just... forget you exist. You're not in their daily life (because you don't work). You're not at social events (because pain/mobility issues prevent attendance). You don't show up on their radar.

And once you're invisible, breaking back into visibility requires enormous energy—energy I often don't have because chronic pain, disability, and bipolar disorder have depleted my reserves.

Strategies to Enhance Social Networks

Expanding and nurturing your social circle is akin to cultivating a garden; it requires patience, effort, and a bit of creativity. Start by exploring new interests or rekindling past passions---join a book club, enroll in a cooking class, or attend community events where you can meet people with similar interests. Such activities not only enrich your social life but also stimulate your mind and keep you engaged with the world around you. Online communities also offer a plethora of opportunities for connection. Platforms dedicated to specific hobbies, professional networking sites, or local community groups can provide valuable social interactions and help build a support system, even from the comfort of your home.

What "enhancing your social network" looks like when you're disabled and invisible:

"Join a book club":

- Requires the ability to leave the house (limited by pain and mobility)
- Requires reliable attendance (can't guarantee I won't be in too much pain or having a bipolar episode)
- Requires energy for social interaction (depleted by managing pain, disability, medications)
- Costs money (even "free" clubs often meet at cafes where you're expected to buy something)

"Enroll in a cooking class":

- Requires standing for extended periods (my shoulder can't handle it)
- Requires the ability to use both arms fully (I can't)
- Requires disposable income (I don't have)
- Assumes you have transportation (limited)

"Attend community events":

- Which ones are wheelchair/mobility device friendly?
- Which ones accommodate chronic pain (seating, breaks, ability to leave early)?

- Which ones don't require standing or prolonged physical activity?
- Which ones can afford when I'm on disability income?

Online communities (the one that actually works):

This is where most of my social connection happens. Writing communities. Online forums. Social media groups for people with similar conditions or interests.

Why online works:

- I can participate from home (no physical barriers)
- I can engage when I have energy (not on a fixed schedule)
- I can be invisible when needed (don't have to explain why I'm absent)
- Usually free (affordable on disability income)
- Accommodates bipolar episodes (can step away during mania or depression without explanation)

But online connection has limitations:

- No physical touch, no in-person presence
- Easy for people to ghost or disappear
- Can feel performative (everyone showing their "best" self)
- Doesn't replace human contact fully
- Can reinforce isolation (never leaving the house)

The irrelevance piece:

When you're not working, when you're disabled, when you're over 50 and female, many social spaces implicitly communicate: "You don't belong here."

Not through explicit exclusion. Through assumptions. Through conversations about careers I can't have, activities I can't do, expenses I can't afford, energy I can't sustain.

I become irrelevant to conversations about professional advancement, travel plans, active hobbies, and financial investments. My reality (disability, pain, limited income, bipolar management) doesn't fit the narrative of "successful aging" most communities celebrate.

What I've learned:

I have to create my own relevance. Find communities where my reality IS the conversation—disability communities, mental health communities, chronic pain communities, writing communities where my experience matters.

But even there, I'm often invisible. Because within disability communities, I'm "not disabled enough." Within bipolar communities, I'm "too functional." Within chronic pain communities, I don't fit clean categories.

Invisibility follows me everywhere.

Leveraging Technology for Connection

In the digital age, technology serves as a bridge over the gap of physical distance, allowing for immediate and often meaningful communication. Tools such as social media, video calls, and instant messaging enable you to maintain close contact with friends and family, regardless of geographical distance. These technologies can be particularly beneficial for those who face mobility challenges or live in remote areas. Regular video chats, for example, can help you stay visually and emotionally connected with your loved ones, providing a sense of closeness that voice calls or text messages cannot fully replicate.

Technology IS my primary connection to the world.

What works:

- Video calls with my adult children (when schedules align)
- Online writing communities (where I have value as a writer, not as a disabled person)
- Social media connections (curated carefully to avoid toxicity)
- Email correspondence (asynchronous, works with variable energy)

What's hard:

Video calls require me to "perform" being okay—put on clothes that aren't just pajamas, arrange my face into expressions that don't show pain, sit upright (which hurts my shoulder), and engage at the other person's energy level.

Some days I can't do that. Those are the days I'm most isolated, most invisible, most irrelevant—because I can't even perform connection through technology.

The cruel irony:

Technology makes connection possible for disabled people. But it also makes us MORE invisible to the able-bodied world. "We talked on video" becomes a substitute for "we spent time together." The screen mediates everything, and I remain at home, isolated, while life happens elsewhere.

What I'm grateful for:

Without technology, my isolation would be absolute. Video calls with my children. Online communities where I have purpose.

The ability to write and share my work. All of this exists because of technology.

But it's not the same as being SEEN. Being PRESENT. Being RELEVANT in someone's physical world.

Barriers to Social Engagement

While the path to enhanced social engagement may seem straightforward, several barriers can impede your progress. Physical limitations such as mobility issues, chronic pain, or even the lack of transportation can significantly restrict your ability to participate in social activities. Psychological barriers like shyness or social anxiety can also be disheartening. Addressing these challenges may require seeking support from community services for transportation or engaging with a therapist to develop strategies to overcome social anxiety. Additionally, community centers often offer a range of activities specifically designed to accommodate varying physical abilities, ensuring everyone has the opportunity to engage without the fear of limitation.

My actual barriers to social engagement:

Physical:

- Chronic shoulder pain limits the duration of activities
- Can't drive long distances (pain, medication side effects)
- Can't stand for extended periods
- Can't lift, carry, or do physical activities others take for granted
- Fatigue from managing pain reduces available energy for socializing

Psychological:

- Bipolar disorder makes me "unpredictable" (people get uncomfortable)
- Social anxiety (partly from being made to feel invisible/irrelevant)
- Fear of having a manic or depressive episode in public
- Shame about disability (internalized ableism is real)
- Anticipation of rejection (why try when you'll be dismissed anyway?)

Financial:

- Can't afford most social activities (restaurants, events, classes)
- Can't reciprocate invitations (can't afford to host or treat others)
- Transportation costs money I don't have
- Even "free" events often have hidden costs

Systemic:

- Ableism (spaces not designed for disabled bodies)
- Ageism (dismissal of older women)
- Mental health stigma (bipolar = "crazy" = avoid)
- Economic exclusion (poverty is invisibility)

The compounding effect:

Each barrier alone would be manageable. Together, they create a fortress of isolation I can't climb out of through individual effort.

"Seeking support from community services" assumes those services exist, are accessible, are affordable, and actually help. Often they don't meet all those criteria.

"Engaging with a therapist to develop strategies" assumes I can afford therapy (I can't, beyond what insurance barely covers), assumes a therapist understands the intersection of disability/bipolar/chronic pain/poverty (rare), assumes strategies CAN overcome systemic barriers (they can't always).

The invisibility/irrelevance trap:

The more barriers you face, the more isolated you become.

The more isolated you become, the more invisible you are.

The more invisible you are, the more irrelevant society considers you.

The more irrelevant you're considered, the fewer resources are directed to helping you.

The fewer resources, the harder it is to overcome barriers.

And the cycle continues.

Interactive Element: Reflective Journaling Prompt

To further enhance your understanding of your social needs and track your progress in building social connections, consider maintaining a reflective journal. Regularly jot down your social interactions, how they made you feel, and what you might want to change going forward. This practice not only provides insight into the types of interactions that fulfill you but also encourages a proactive approach to seeking out and nurturing relationships that contribute positively to your emotional well-being. Be careful with journaling. I became addicted to Pinterest because I started creating my own journals!

By recognizing the signs of isolation early, actively seeking enriching social interactions, leveraging technology for connectivity, and overcoming barriers to social engagement, you set the stage for a richer, more connected life. These strategies, though simple in concept, require deliberate action and adjustment tailored to your personal circumstances and needs. As you implement these strategies, remember that the quality of your social connections can significantly influence not only your emotional health but also your physical health and overall happiness.

5.2 The Impact of Pets on Aging and Emotional Health

The companionship of a pet can often be one of life's greatest joys, providing not just company but also a plethora of emotional and physical benefits, particularly as you age. The presence of a pet can lead to increased physical activity; for instance, walking a dog regularly encourages regular exercise, which strengthens the heart, tones muscles, and can significantly improve your overall physical health. Beyond the physical, pets offer a remarkable source of comfort and emotional support. They provide unconditional love and acceptance, which can be incredibly soothing, reducing stress and anxiety. Interacting with pets has been shown to raise levels of serotonin and dopamine, neurotransmitters that play a part in calming and relaxation. This effect can be particularly profound for older adults dealing with loneliness or depression, as pets offer companionship that can alleviate feelings of isolation.

Choosing the right pet is crucial and should be based on your lifestyle, physical ability, and personal preferences. For those who enjoy regular walks and have a relatively active lifestyle, a dog might be a suitable option. However, if you prefer a less demanding companion, cats, which require less active engagement, can be ideal. It is also vital to consider your living arrangements and any allergies you might have. For instance, birds or fish can be wonderful pets for someone who may not have the ability to walk a dog or for someone living in a smaller space. Each type of pet brings its unique benefits and requires a different level of care, so considering these factors will help ensure that your pet enhances your life.

Managing the responsibilities of pet ownership is an important consideration as one ages. Pets require not just love and attention but also regular feeding, grooming, and visits to the vet, which can become challenging as one's mobility decreases or if health issues arise. Planning for these responsibilities is essential. One strategy is to engage pet care services that can provide assistance with walking, feeding, or even daycare for pets. Another option is to consider community resources such as local animal shelters or pet clubs that can offer support or advice. Additionally, technology can aid pet care through automatic feeders or video systems that allow you to monitor your pet while away from home.

For those unable to own pets, there are valuable alternatives that can still provide the benefits of animal companionship. Volunteering at an animal shelter or participating in pet therapy programs are excellent options. These activities not only allow you to interact with animals but also provide opportunities to meet and connect with other animal lovers, enriching your social life. Pet therapy, especially, has been recognized for its psychological benefits, often used in settings like nursing homes or hospitals to bring joy and comfort to those who may not be able to own pets themselves.

I don't have pets currently. This is a deliberate choice based on my limitations.

Why I can't have a dog (which I'd love):

- Can't walk a dog regularly (pain, mobility, energy)
- Can't afford vet care, food, supplies (disability income)
- Can't physically control a dog if it pulls (shoulder limitations)
- Can't guarantee consistent care during bipolar episodes

Why I can't have a cat (also would love):

- Litter box management requires bending, lifting (my shoulder)
- Vet care costs (can't afford)
- My husband is allergic
- Can't guarantee consistent care during severe depression

The loss this represents:

Pets provide unconditional love, routine, purpose, physical touch, and companionship—all things I desperately need and don't have enough of.

Not having pets adds to isolation. Removes a potential source of connection. Eliminates daily structure and purpose.

But I can't manage the responsibility with my physical and mental health limitations. And acknowledging that feels like another failure, another way I'm "less than," another piece of evidence that I'm irrelevant.

The irony: Research shows pets reduce isolation and improve emotional health, especially for older adults. But accessing that benefit requires resources and capabilities I don't have. Another thing designed to help people "like me" that I can't actually use.

Embracing the company of pets or engaging with animals through alternative means can significantly enrich your life, offering joy, companionship, and numerous health benefits. Whether through direct ownership or other forms of interaction, the bond between humans and animals continues to be a powerful source of emotional and physical well-being, particularly impactful as you navigate the later stages of life.

5.3 Volunteering: Connecting with Community for Purpose and Joy

The act of volunteering---offering your time and skills to help others---is much more than a noble endeavor; it's a profound way to enrich your own life. Engaging in volunteer activities can imbue your days with purpose, elevate your self-esteem, and expand your social horizons. When you volunteer, you're not just giving; you're also receiving. This reciprocity creates a cycle of positivity that enhances both individual lives and the broader community.

Volunteering can significantly fortify your sense of purpose. In a phase of life where professional responsibilities might be winding down or personal projects may no longer occupy much of your time, finding new purposes is essential. Volunteer activities can fill this void, offering tasks that challenge you and make a tangible difference in others' lives. This sense of purpose is linked closely with improved mental health; it provides a reason to get up in the morning, something to look forward to, and a role that adds meaning to your life. Besides, feeling useful counters any societal messages about aging that focus on decline rather than growth. Studies consistently show that having a sense of purpose can decrease the risk of disease, improve life satisfaction, and even extend lifespan.

Another significant benefit of volunteering is the enhancement of self-esteem. Completing tasks, helping others, and seeing the results of your efforts can boost your confidence. This boost is particularly impactful during a life stage when many might struggle with self-worth due to retirement or physical limitations brought about by aging. Volunteering reaffirms your capabilities and worth, highlighting the valuable contributions you can still make, regardless of age.

Social connections are naturally woven into the fabric of volunteer activities. Whether you're working alongside others at a food bank, teaching skills to younger generations, or organizing community events, each interaction contributes to a network of relationships. These social connections are vital, providing emotional support, reducing feelings of loneliness, and increasing your sense of community belonging. Engaging regularly with a diverse group of individuals, both old and young, also promotes an exchange of ideas and perspectives, keeping your social skills sharp and your mind open.

I'm not "retired." I'm disabled. There's a difference.

Retirement implies choice, planning, transition from working to not-working with financial security and agency.

Disability is a forced exit from work, financial precarity, loss of identity, and sudden irrelevance in a productivity-obsessed culture.

The "purpose" question haunts me:

When your worth was tied to work, and you can no longer work, what are you worth?

When your identity was professional, and that identity is gone, who are you?

When your purpose was productivity, and you're no longer productive, why do you matter?

Society's answers are crushing:

You don't matter. You're a drain. You're irrelevant. You're invisible.

What I've had to learn:

My purpose isn't external validation. It's not productivity. It's not an economic contribution.

My purpose NOW:

- Writing (this book, others)—sharing what I've learned so others don't have to learn it the hard way
- Being a mother to my adult children—presence, love, support
- Being a wife to my husband—a partnership despite everything
- Processing my experiences through art, journaling, andcontent creation
- Learning (German, always more to learn)
- Surviving each day despite pain, disability, and bipolar episodes

Is this "enough" purpose? Society says no. I'm still learning to say yes.

The invisibility of this purpose:

None of it shows up on résumés. None of it earns money. None of it impresses people at social gatherings. None of it makes me visible or relevant in conventional terms.

But it's real. It matters. Even if only to me.

About volunteering specifically:

I can't volunteer in traditional ways. Can't commit to regular schedules (bipolar/pain variability). Can't do physical tasks (shoulder limitations). Can't afford transportation to volunteer sites. Can't guarantee I'll show up consistently (disability reality).

This feels like another failure. Another way I'm "less than." Another door closed because my body/mind/finances don't cooperate.

But I volunteer in ways that work for me: answering questions in online writing communities, sharing knowledge when I can, supporting other people with bipolar disorder or chronic pain when I have capacity.

It's not conventional volunteering. It won't show up on any official records. But it's a real contribution. Even if invisible.

Finding the Right Opportunity

Identifying the right volunteering opportunity that aligns with your passions, skills, and physical capabilities is crucial for a fulfilling experience. Start by considering what you are passionate about. Is it education, environment, health, or community development? Local nonprofits, schools, and community centers often look for volunteers with a range of interests and skills. Many organizations post their needs on their websites or on platforms like VolunteerMatch, which can help you find opportunities that match your interests in your locality.

Reflect on what skills you can offer. Are you a retired teacher, a seasoned gardener, or perhaps a skilled carpenter? Many organizations need diverse skills — from teaching to gardening to administrative support. Your career skills can be highly beneficial, but personal hobbies and interests are equally valuable. As well, consider your physical capabilities. If mobility is a concern, many organizations offer roles that can be performed remotely, such as virtual tutoring or administrative work from home.

Once you've pinpointed an area of interest and assessed your skills, reach out to organizations to learn more about their volunteer programs. Don't hesitate to ask questions about the commitments involved. Some roles may require a regular weekly schedule, while others might be project-based or seasonal. Ensure the volunteering schedule aligns with your lifestyle and health needs, providing a balance that enriches rather than exhausts.

Impact on Well-being

Engaging in volunteer work not only enriches your community, but also significantly boosts your own mental and emotional health. Research and case studies have illuminated the profound impact volunteering has on reducing symptoms of depression and loneliness. A study by the Corporation for National and Community Service reports a strong relationship between volunteering and health: those who volunteer have lower mortality rates, greater functional ability, and lower rates of depression later in life than those who do not volunteer. The social interaction and sense of accomplishment that come with volunteer activities can elevate your mood and outlook on life, providing a healthy buffer against the psychological challenges of aging.

Volunteering also offers a unique avenue for social interaction, serving as a bridge to meeting new people and strengthening community ties. This aspect of volunteering is especially beneficial for those who may feel disconnected or isolated. Through regular interactions with fellow volunteers and community members, you build meaningful relationships that foster a sense of belonging and community engagement. These relationships can be particularly sustaining, offering emotional support and camaraderie.

In essence, volunteering provides a pathway to a richer, more connected life. It offers a way to continue growing, learning, and contributing, thereby enhancing your sense of self and your engagement with the world. As you invest your time and energy into volunteer activities, you not only make a positive impact on the community but also pave the way for a fulfilling, joy-filled life.

5.4 Managing Grief and Loss as You Age

Grief is a multifaceted response to loss, particularly to the loss of someone or something to which a bond was formed. As we age, the experiences of loss become more frequent---not only through the death of peers and partners but also through the loss of independence and other significant life changes. Understanding that grief is a natural process that everyone navigates differently is crucial. It manifests in various forms: sadness, anger, disbelief, or even relief, all of which are normal reactions. Particularly for older adults, these losses can feel compounded as they happen more frequently and can include friends, siblings, and significant others.

The process of grieving can profoundly affect both your mental and physical health. It's not uncommon to experience sleep disruptions, changes in appetite, or decreased motivation during periods of mourning. However, there are healthy ways to cope with grief that can ease the pain and help you move toward recovery. Engaging in support groups can be particularly beneficial. These groups provide a safe space to share your feelings with others who are experiencing similar losses, which can be incredibly comforting and reduce feelings of isolation. If group settings are not comfortable for you, one-on-one counseling with a therapist who specializes in grief can also provide significant support, offering professional guidance to help you navigate your emotions and find ways to cope.

In addition to professional help, immersing yourself in activities that bring you joy is essential. Whether it's gardening, painting, or listening to music, these activities can provide a meaningful distraction from your grief, helping to manage the intensity of your emotions. Engaging in physical activity, such as walking or yoga, can also have therapeutic effects. Exercise releases endorphins, which are chemicals in the brain that act as natural painkillers. It also improves the ability to sleep, which in turn reduces stress.

Maintaining connections with loved ones who are lost is another key aspect of healing. Creating a memorial or engaging in legacy work, such as compiling photo albums, writing stories, or planting a garden in their memory, can provide a constructive outlet for your grief and help keep your loved ones' memories alive. These acts of remembrance can be powerful tools for emotional healing, allowing you to honor those you have lost while expressing your feelings in a tangible way.

Preparing for inevitable losses is also a practical aspect of managing grief. This can include having open discussions with family members about end-of-life wishes, which can ensure that your loved ones' desires are respected and reduce family stress during what will undoubtedly be a difficult time. Legal preparations, such as creating wills or establishing living trusts, can also alleviate potential conflicts or confusion, ensuring that the focus remains on mourning and healing rather than on logistical or financial concerns.

I'm grieving losses people don't acknowledge as "real" grief:

Loss of career: Forced retirement at 56 feels like death. The professional identity I built over decades is gone. People don't understand this as grief—"you get to relax now!" No. I lost purpose, income, identity, and relevance.

Loss of physical capability: Mourning what my body used to do. Activities I'll never do again. Independence I'll never regain. This is ambiguous grief—the loss of who I was, who I could have been.

Loss of future possibilities: At almost 60, disabled, I know certain futures will never happen. Travel I wanted to do. Careers I might have pursued. Financial security I'll never achieve. These aren't dramatic losses, but they hurt.

Loss of relevance: Watching yourself become invisible is a kind of death. You're still here, but you don't matter the same way. Society has decided you're past your expiration date.

The complicated grief of bipolar disorder:

During depressive episodes, I grieve EVERYTHING—past losses, current situation, future impossibilities, my entire existence. This grief is pathological, not proportional, but it's still real.

During manic episodes, grief disappears—everything is brilliant, possible, fixable. This isn't healthy either.

Finding balanced grief—acknowledging losses without being consumed by them—requires stability I don't always have.

What helps:

- Writing about losses (processing through words)
- Art journaling (expressing what words can't)
- Talking to my husband (when I can articulate it)
- Accepting that grief comes in waves (some days manageable, some not)

What doesn't help:

- "At least you have disability income" (minimizes loss)
- "You're lucky you don't have to work" (misses the point entirely)
- "Find a new purpose" (as if purpose is replaceable, interchangeable)
- "Stay positive" (toxic positivity that denies real grief)

The invisibility of ambiguous grief:

When someone dies, society acknowledges your grief. When your career dies, your body fails, your future narrows—society tells you to "move on," "stay positive," "find new purpose."

Your grief is invisible because your losses are invisible. You're grieving things other people can't see, don't value, don't understand.

And that makes the grief harder. Because you're alone in it. Invisible in your sorrow.

By understanding the natural process of grief, utilizing healthy coping mechanisms, maintaining connections with those who have passed, and preparing for future losses, you can navigate these challenging times with grace and flexibility. These strategies not only help manage the pain associated with grief but also foster a sense of peace and acceptance, allowing you to move forward with a continued appreciation for life and the relationships that make it meaningful.

5.5 The Benefits of Laughter and Lightheartedness

Laughter, often heard as the joyful sound at gatherings, has profound effects that go beyond mere expressions of happiness. It acts as a powerful antidote to stress, pain, and conflict. Nothing works faster or more dependably to bring your mind and body back into balance than a good laugh. Humor lightens your burdens, inspires hope, connects you to others, and keeps you grounded, focused, and alert. It also helps you release anger and forgive sooner. When you start to laugh, it doesn't just lighten your mental load; it actually triggers physical changes in your body. Laughter enhances your intake of oxygen-rich air, stimulates your heart, lungs, and muscles, and increases the endorphins that are released by your brain. This leads to a general sense of well-being and can temporarily relieve pain. Furthermore, laughter can also stimulate circulation and aid muscle relaxation, both of which can help reduce some of the physical symptoms of stress.

Long-term effects include improvements in your immune system. Negative thoughts manifest into chemical reactions that can affect your body by bringing more stress into your system and decreasing your immunity. In contrast, positive thoughts can actually release neuropeptides that help fight stress and potentially more serious illnesses. One study found that people with a strong sense of humor lived longer than those who didn't laugh as much. The difference was particularly notable for those battling cancer.

Laughter is complicated when you're dealing with chronic pain, disability, and bipolar disorder.

During stable periods:

Laughter genuinely helps. Reduces stress. Provides physical relief (endorphins). Connects me to my husband and others. Makes life bearable.

I watch comedy. Share funny stories. Find humor in the absurdity of my situation. Laugh at myself, at life, at the ridiculous challenges disability creates.

During depressive episodes:

Nothing is funny. Laughter feels impossible, foreign, like something other people do. Comedy shows irritate me. Humor feels cruel. I can't access joy.

During manic episodes:

Everything is hilarious. I laugh inappropriately, excessively. The mania creates a kind of euphoric humor that's not... healthy. It's not balanced joy—it's pathological.

With chronic pain:

Laughter literally hurts sometimes. Deep laughter engages core muscles, moves my shoulder, and creates physical pain. So I have to moderate even joy—can't laugh too hard or I'll pay for it.

The invisibility of conditional joy:

People don't understand why I can't just "choose happiness" or "find humor" on demand. They don't see that my ability to laugh is gated by:

- Current mood state (bipolar)
- Pain levels (physical)
- Energy reserves (depleted by managing conditions)
- Medication effects (some reduce emotional range)

What works for me:

- Gentle humor during stable periods
- Dark comedy that acknowledges suffering (not toxic positivity)
- Self-deprecating jokes about disability (reclaiming power through humor)
- Shared laughter with my husband (intimacy through joy)

What doesn't work:

- Forced cheerfulness ("just smile!")
- Humor that mocks disability or mental illness
- Pressure to "lighten up" during depression
- Manic "humor" that's actually symptom not joy

Using humor to cope with invisibility:

Sometimes the only way to deal with being invisible is to joke about it. "I'm so insignificant I could rob a bank and no one would notice." Dark? Yes. But it takes back power. Makes the invisibility less crushing.

Humor about irrelevance. About disability. About bipolar disorder. About chronic pain. About poverty. About being dismissed by society.

Not because it's funny. But laughing at it hurts less than crying about it.

And sometimes, that's the best I can do.

Incorporating Humor into Daily Life

To incorporate more humor and laughter into your life, start by seeking out fun activities that make you laugh. Attend a comedy club, watch a funny movie or TV show, or go to a comedy night. Even merely sharing a good joke or a funny story with others can be an effective way to increase laughter. You could also try playing games with friends and family that incorporate humor and light-hearted competition, such as charades or board games that encourage playful interaction.

Laughter yoga is another potent method to introduce more laughter into your life. It combines simulated laughter exercises with gentle breathing techniques to cultivate joy and health. Practicing laughter yoga regularly can significantly boost your mood and improve your resilience against stress. Classes are available at many community centers and on online platforms, making them accessible to a broad audience. Do not feel bad. This is almost too woowoo for me and I'm convinced some of the practices work for me.

Social Benefits of Laughter

Laughter is contagious; it binds people together and increases happiness and intimacy. Laughter also creates and strengthens relationships. In social contexts, shared laughter is one of the most effective tools for keeping relationships fresh and exciting. All emotional sharing builds strong and lasting relationship bonds, but sharing laughter and play also adds joy, vitality, and resilience. Additionally, laughter is a powerful, natural antidote to stress, conflict, and pain. By incorporating humor and laughter into your interactions, you can improve the quality of your social interactions and deepen your relationships.

Using Humor to Navigate Aging

As you age, embracing humor can be a vital tool in dealing with life's inevitable challenges. Using humor to cope with the frustrations of aging can transform potential obstacles into opportunities for joy and laughter. For instance, joking about forgetfulness or the mix-ups of daily life can help keep the atmosphere light and reduce stress. Humor can also help you connect with others who are going through similar experiences, providing mutual support and encouragement to face the challenges of aging with a positive outlook.

By integrating laughter and humor into your daily routine, you enhance your own well-being and enrich your interactions with others. Laughter is a universal language that everyone understands. It can bridge gaps, heal hearts, and renew hope. Embracing laughter is embracing life, with all its twists and turns, ups and downs, and not merely surviving but thriving because of them.

As this chapter closes, I want to acknowledge something the research often overlooks:

Emotional well-being and social connection aren't just about individual effort.

You can do everything "right"—join communities, leverage technology, find purpose, process grief, cultivate humor—and still be isolated. Still be invisible. Still be irrelevant in society's eyes.

Because some isolation is structural, not personal, some invisibility is systemic, not chosen. Some irrelevance is imposed by a society that values productivity over humanity.

This doesn't mean the strategies don't help. They do. Every connection matters. Every moment of purpose counts. Every genuine laugh helps.

But they can't "fix" the fundamental problem: that society renders certain people invisible and irrelevant based on age, disability, mental illness, gender, and economic status.

What I've learned:

Create visibility for yourself: Even if society doesn't see you, YOU see you. Your experiences matter. Your reality is valid. Your existence has worth.

Find communities that value you: Not "mainstream" communities that see you as deficient, but communities where your reality is the norm, your experiences are shared, and your presence is valued.

Accept that some days you'll be invisible: Fighting it every moment is exhausting. Some days, just survive. Invisibility isn't permanent even when it feels that way.

Build connections where possible: Online. With family. With communities that get it. Connection doesn't have to be conventional to be real.

Define your own relevance: Society's definition is broken. You get to decide what makes you matter. For me, it's writing, learning, loving, surviving. That's enough.

The fear of invisibility, irrelevance, and isolation will never fully go away when you're disabled, mentally ill, older, female, and poor in a society that devalues all those things.

But you can live despite the fear. Create meaning despite invisibility. Connect despite isolation. Matter despite irrelevance.

Not because society validates it. But because YOU know it's true.

At 58, invisible to most of the world but visible to myself, I'm still here. Still writing. Still learning. Still surviving.

That's nothing. Even when society pretends it is.

Chapter 6: Lifestyle Adjustments for Age Optimization

I can't control my own life anymore.

That's the reality of disability at my age. My body makes decisions that override my preferences. My finances dictate choices that used to be mine to make. My limitations set boundaries I never agreed to.

Loss of autonomy isn't abstract—it's my daily reality:

My shoulder decides when I can work (never, apparently). My bipolar disorder decides when I'm stable enough to engage with the world. My chronic pain decides what activities are possible on any given day. My disability income decides what I can afford, where I can live, and what opportunities are available.

I don't get to choose based on what I want. I choose based on what my body allows and what my bank account permits.

And underneath all of it is the terror:

The fear that I'll become indigent. That disability income won't be enough. That one major expense will push me over the edge into poverty I can't recover from. That I'll end up homeless, dependent on charity, invisible even to the social safety net that's supposed to catch people like me.

This fear isn't irrational. I watch my bank account. I know how little margin I have. One emergency—medical, housing, anything— and I'm in crisis.

The intersection of lost autonomy and financial vulnerability creates a trap:

I can't improve my financial situation because my body won't let me work. I can't address my physical limitations because I can't afford the treatments, equipment, or support that might help. Each limitation reinforces the other, creating a cage I can't escape through individual effort.

This chapter is about lifestyle adjustments for age optimization—decluttering, technology, home safety, travel, fashion, all designed to help you age well and maintain independence.

The advice is solid. The research is sound. The strategies work.

But they're written for people with resources. With choices. With autonomy over their lives and finances.

I'm going to share the science of lifestyle optimization. But I'm also going to tell you what it's like when you don't have the money to implement these strategies, when your body won't cooperate with the recommendations, when autonomy is something you lost years ago and financial security is a fantasy.

Because the gap between "what you should do" and "what you can actually do" is where real life happens. And pretending that gap doesn't exist helps no one.

Let me show you both: the ideal strategies AND the reality of limited resources and lost control.

6.1 Decluttering for Clarity and Ease in Later Years

Benefits of Decluttering

The act of decluttering goes beyond mere cleaning or organizing; it's a process that can significantly reduce stress and enhance your living environment. A clutter-free home reduces the time and energy spent on cleaning and maintenance, allowing more room for restorative activities that enrich your life. More importantly, decluttering minimizes the risk of accidents. As mobility and balance may become concerns with age, ensuring clear pathways and easily accessible essentials can make a substantial difference to daily safety. The psychological benefits are equally profound. A tidy and organized space can lead to a more peaceful mind, reducing feelings of anxiety and overwhelm that often accompany cluttered environments. This mental clarity is crucial as it enhances your ability to make decisions, focus on your health, and engage more fully with life.

I can't declutter effectively because my shoulder won't let me.

The physical act of sorting, lifting, moving, and organizing—all require abilities I don't have. I can't lift boxes. Can't reach high shelves. Can't carry things to the donation centers. Can't reorganize heavy furniture.

What decluttering looks like with physical limitations:

I can sort items into piles (keep, donate, trash). That's about it. Then I need help—my husband, when he has time—to actually move things, carry things, dispose of things.

The autonomy piece:

I don't get to declutter on MY schedule. I have to wait until someone can help me. My space remains cluttered not because I don't know it's beneficial, but because I physically can't execute the solution.

The financial piece:

Donation services that pick up items? Cost money or require you to have significant items worth their time. Hiring someone to help? Can't afford it. Storage solutions (clear boxes, organizational systems)? Every dollar counts when you're on disability income.

The cruel irony:

A cluttered space increases stress and accident risk—both things that make my conditions worse. But addressing the clutter requires physical capability and financial resources I don't have.

So I live with clutter that I know is harmful, unable to fix it, watching it contribute to the very problems (stress, safety hazards) that the research warns about.

This isn't laziness. This isn't "not trying." This is a loss of autonomy—my environment is controlling me instead of me controlling my environment.

Step-by-Step Decluttering Guide

Starting the decluttering process can feel harrowing, particularly if many years' worth of belongings have accumulated. The key is to start small — one drawer, one closet, or one room at a time. Begin by categorizing items into those you need and use regularly, those you might need occasionally, and those you haven't used in over a year. This simple yet effective categorization can help you objectively assess what to keep and what to let go of. For many, sentimental items can be the hardest to manage. In these cases, consider keeping only a few cherished mementos and photographing others before letting them go, preserving the memories without keeping the physical clutter.

Tools and Methods for Effective Decluttering

Certain tools and methods can be incredibly helpful in facilitating the decluttering process. For instance, using clear, labeled boxes for storage can help you maintain order and easily locate items when they're needed. For items that are no longer needed but still in good condition, donation services offer a way to declutter while helping others. Many charities will even pick up items from your home, making the process easier and more rewarding. Online selling platforms like eBay or Facebook Marketplace are great for items that may have financial value. This clears your space and offers a potential income source. For documents and paperwork, consider digital solutions — scanning and storing files electronically can dramatically reduce physical clutter and make important documents easier to manage and access.

Online selling platforms offer a potential income source"—in theory.

In practice:

Taking photos requires positioning items, which I can't always do with shoulder limitations. Writing descriptions, managing listings, responding to buyers, packaging items, and getting them to shipping locations—all require time, energy, and physical capability.

I've tried selling things online and made maybe $50 total over months of effort. The return on investment (time, energy, pain from physical activity) wasn't worth it.

The financial desperation piece:

I NEED that potential income. Every dollar matters when you're on disability. But I can't generate it efficiently enough to make it worthwhile.

This is the loss of autonomy: knowing there's money in my possessions I could extract, but my body won't cooperate with the process of extraction.

Maintaining a Decluttered Space

Once you've achieved a decluttered home, the challenge shifts to maintaining this new state. Adopting minimalist habits can be key; before acquiring a new item, ask yourself if it's truly necessary or if it might add to clutter. Regular reviews of your space, perhaps seasonally or annually, can help catch clutter before it accumulates. Another effective strategy is to implement a 'one in, one out' rule, particularly for areas like clothing or kitchen gadgets. When a new item comes in, an old one goes out, preventing the gradual accumulation of belongings. This keeps your space clear and encourages thoughtful purchasing, enhancing your overall quality of life.

"Thoughtful purchasing" assumes you have purchasing power.

When you're on disability income, you're not acquiring new items regularly. You're desperately trying to make what you have last as long as possible.

The "one in, one out" rule is irrelevant when "one in" happens maybe twice a year and only when something breaks beyond repair.

What "maintaining a decluttered space" actually means for me:

Trying not to let things pile up when I don't have the energy to put them away. Asking my husband to help move things before clutter accumulates. Feeling guilty that I can't maintain my own space independently.

Loss of autonomy, again. My environment controls me.

Reflective Journaling Prompt

To deepen your understanding and commitment to a decluttered lifestyle, consider maintaining a decluttering journal. This can be a space to reflect on what you've removed from your home and how these changes have affected your daily life and mental well-being. Reflect on questions like, "How does the space make me feel now?" or "What have I learned about my needs and habits through this process?" This practice not only reinforces the benefits of decluttering but also integrates the principles of simplicity and mindfulness into your everyday life.

By embracing decluttering, you're not just cleaning out a home; you're paving a pathway toward a more intentional and fulfilling lifestyle. This process of external simplification can often lead to profound internal discoveries, allowing you to live more fully in the present and prepare thoughtfully for the future.

6.2 The Role of Technology in Aging: Helpful Tools and Resources

In an era where technology is at the forefront of innovation, its integration into the aging process presents a myriad of benefits that can significantly enhance your quality of life. From wearable devices that monitor health metrics to applications that keep your mind engaged, technology offers tools that not only maintain but also improve your physical and cognitive abilities.

Technological Tools for Health Monitoring

Imagine a scenario where your daily health metrics, such as heart rate, sleep patterns, and physical activity levels, are seamlessly tracked and analyzed. Wearable fitness trackers and health monitoring apps play a pivotal role in making this a reality. Devices like Fitbit or apps such as Apple Health allow you to keep a close eye on your vital statistics, providing data that can be invaluable for managing chronic conditions or adjusting your fitness regimen. The convenience of having these tools at your fingertips encourages a proactive approach to health management, enabling you to make informed decisions about your lifestyle. For instance, noticing a consistent dip in sleep quality might prompt you to adjust your evening routine or seek medical advice. The empowerment that comes from having real-time data about your body's functioning is remarkable, offering a sense of control that is particularly reassuring as you age.

"The empowerment that comes from having real-time data"— if you can afford the devices.

Fitbits cost money. Apple Watches cost a significant amount of money. Even fitness apps often have premium features behind paywalls.

What I can afford:

My smartphone (which I already had). Free apps with limited functionality. That's it.

The data I actually get:

Basic step counting (often inaccurate because I'm not walking smoothly due to pain). Sleep tracking (tells me what I already know: I sleep poorly). Heart rate monitoring (sometimes, when the phone cooperates).

What I DON'T get:

Detailed health metrics that require expensive wearables. Professional analysis of patterns. Integration with healthcare providers (which requires specific devices). The "empowerment" described above.

The financial vulnerability piece:

Every recommendation assumes disposable income. Assumes you can buy a $200-400 device plus monthly subscription fees for premium features. Assumes technology is an investment you can afford.

For me, technology isn't empowerment—it's a reminder of what I can't access because I can't afford it.

Loss of autonomy:

I can't take control of my health through technology because I can't afford the tools. My financial limitations dictate my health management options.

Safety Enhancements Through Technology

As you navigate the later years, safety becomes a paramount concern, particularly if you cherish your independence. Advanced technologies such as emergency response systems and GPS trackers can provide peace of mind not just for you but also for your loved ones. Devices like medical alert systems, often worn as necklaces or bracelets, ensure that help is just a button press away should you experience a fall or sudden health issue. Similarly, GPS trackers can be integrated into phones or watches, offering real-time location data---a feature that is incredibly useful if you enjoy walking or if you're managing conditions like early-stage dementia. These technologies respect your desire for independence while ensuring that safety is always within reach, blending security with freedom in your daily life.

Medical alert systems: $30-50/month minimum.

When your disability income is limited, $30/month for a medical alert system means $30 less for food, utilities, medications, or emergency savings.

The financial calculation I actually make:

Can I afford to fall and not be found quickly? No.

Can I afford $30-50/month for a system? Also no.

So I don't have one. I'm dependent on my husband being home or hoping my phone is within reach if something happens.

This is what financial vulnerability feels like:

Knowing there's a solution that would help, knowing you need it, knowing you can't afford it. Choosing between safety and eating. Between security and keeping the lights on.

Loss of autonomy:

My finances decide my safety level. Not my preferences. Not my needs. My bank account.

Staying Connected

The importance of maintaining social connections as you age cannot be overstated, and technology provides numerous tools to enhance your ability to stay in touch. Social media platforms like Facebook or Instagram allow you to keep up with friends and family, sharing moments and memories across any distance. Video chat apps such as Skype or Zoom can help bridge the gap even further, offering face-to-face interactions that are invaluable for those with family members who live far away. Online community forums provide spaces to connect with peers who share similar interests or are navigating similar life stages, offering support and camaraderie that can be invaluable for emotional well-being. These tools ensure that maintaining social ties does not have to diminish with physical distance, allowing you to nurture relationships that are vital for your mental health.

Technology for connection DOES work for me—it's the one area where free options exist.

Free video calls. Free social media. Free online communities. This is where technology actually serves people without money.

But even here, there are limits: reliable internet costs money. Newer devices work better. Data plans have limits.

I'm grateful for what I have access to. But I'm aware that even this could disappear if I can't afford internet service.

Technology for Cognitive Engagement

Keeping your mind sharp as you age is essential, and technology offers a plethora of resources to stimulate cognitive activity. Educational apps, online courses, and even virtual reality experiences can provide engaging ways to learn new information and skills, from foreign languages to historical events. Platforms like Coursera or Khan Academy offer courses on a wide range of topics, often for free, allowing you to explore subjects that interest you from the comfort of your home. For a more immersive experience, virtual reality systems can transport you to virtual worlds where learning comes alive, whether it's walking through a digitally reconstructed ancient city or exploring the human body in 3D. These technological tools make learning not only accessible but also exciting, providing stimulating mental activities that can keep your cognitive faculties in top form.

Free online courses are genuinely accessible and I use them.

This is one recommendation I CAN follow. Learning German through free apps and websites. Taking free courses when I have energy.

Virtual reality? Not happening.

VR systems cost hundreds to thousands of dollars. That's not accessible on disability income.

The pattern:

Recommendations that assume financial resources create a two-tier system. Those with money get optimal solutions. Those without get whatever free options exist, if any.

By embracing these technological advancements, you equip yourself with tools that enhance your ability to manage your health, maintain safety, foster social connections, and actively engage your mind. This integration of technology into daily life ensures that aging can be navigated not just with ease but with confidence, allowing you to enjoy your later years with the support and enrichment that modern technology provides.

6.3 Redesigning Your Living Space for Safety and Accessibility

Redesigning your living space to enhance safety and accessibility is not only a proactive step towards a more comfortable lifestyle but also an essential measure to ensure independence and well-being as you age. The spaces we inhabit play a significant role in our daily lives, influencing our mobility, mood, and overall health. To begin this process, a thorough assessment of your home is crucial. This evaluation should focus on identifying potential safety hazards that could lead to falls or injuries. Common areas of concern include loose carpeting, inadequate lighting, and cluttered walkways that can impede movement. Additionally, bathrooms and kitchens are high-risk areas due to their typically hard surfaces and potential for wet floors.

Once potential hazards are identified, the next step is to consider specific modifications that can significantly enhance the accessibility and safety of your home. Installing ramps at entryways is a fundamental modification if stairs become a challenge, ensuring easy access for wheelchairs and walkers. Similarly, in bathrooms, grab bars near the toilet and in the shower area can provide the necessary support to prevent slips and falls, one of the most common household accidents among older adults. Stairlifts are another excellent option for homes with multiple levels, enabling you to move safely between floors without the physical strain of climbing stairs.

"Installing ramps... grab bars... stairlifts"—all cost money I don't have.

The financial reality:

- Ramps: $1,000-3,000+ professionally installed
- Grab bars: $50-200+ per bar, plus installation
- Stairlifts: $3,000-5,000+

I'm on disability income. These aren't options. They're fantasies.

What I can afford:

Nothing. I make do with what exists. I navigate stairs carefully, holding railings with my good arm. I don't have grab bars in the shower—I just try not to fall.

The fear:

One fall could hospitalize me. Could create medical bills I can't pay. Could make me even more dependent, even less able to work, even more financially vulnerable.

But I can't afford the modifications that would prevent the fall.

This is the trap:

Financial vulnerability prevents me from addressing safety issues. Safety issues increase the risk of injury/medical crisis. A medical crisis would destroy what little financial stability I have.

Loss of autonomy:

My finances decide my safety. My bank account determines whether I get grab bars, ramps, or accessibility modifications. Not my needs. Not the recommendations. My poverty.

The arrangement of furniture and overall layout of your home also requires careful consideration to improve mobility and prevent accidents. It's advisable to arrange furniture to create clear, wide pathways that allow for easy navigation, especially if mobility aids such as walkers or wheelchairs are used. Consider the height and stability of furniture as well. For example, chairs and sofas should be at a height that makes sitting down and standing up relatively effortless for someone with limited mobility. Adjustable beds and chairs can also offer added comfort and support, adapting to your needs to facilitate rest and relaxation.

Adjustable beds: $1,000-3,000+. Not happening.

I have the furniture I have. It's not optimal for my shoulder, my pain, my mobility. But it's what I can afford (i.e., what I already own).

Improving lighting throughout your home is another critical aspect of creating a safe and accessible environment. Adequate lighting is vital for preventing falls and ensuring that you can perform daily tasks efficiently and safely. Assess each room and passageway to ensure that it is well-lit, paying special attention to areas where tasks are performed, such as the kitchen, bathroom, and any workspace. Consider a mix of overhead lighting, task lighting, and ambient lighting to provide clarity without glare, which can be uncomfortable and disorienting. Nightlights in hallways, bedrooms, and bathrooms are also wise additions, offering gentle illumination that can guide you during nocturnal movements.

LED bulbs and nightlights I CAN afford.

This is one recommendation that's actually accessible. Better lighting is relatively cheap and genuinely helpful.

But even here: the electricity to run lights costs money. Every utility bill matters when you're counting dollars.

Each of these strategies not only enhances the physical safety of your living environment but also promotes a sense of confidence and ease, allowing you to navigate your daily life more freely and comfortably. By taking the time to assess and modify your living space, you create a supportive setting that accommodates your evolving needs, ensuring that your home remains a sanctuary of comfort and accessibility.

6.4 Travel Tips for the Aging Adventurer

Embarking on travel adventures enriches life, offering new experiences and memories that can be particularly rewarding as you navigate the later years. Whether you're a seasoned traveler aiming to explore new destinations or you're planning a leisurely retreat, preparing adequately ensures that your travel experiences are both enjoyable and comfortable.

I don't travel.

Let me be clear about that upfront. Travel requires money I don't have and physical capability I've lost.

The financial reality:

- Airfare: Hundreds to thousands
- Accommodations: Hundreds more
- Food while traveling: Daily expense
- Activities: Additional costs
- Travel insurance: Another expense
- Accessible accommodations: Usually cost MORE

My disability income covers basic living expenses. There's no travel budget. There's no "leisure retreat" fund.

The physical reality:

- Can't carry luggage (shoulder)
- Can't stand in lines for extended periods (pain)
- Can't guarantee stable mood (bipolar makes travel risky)
- Can't predict pain levels days in advance (can't book non-refundable tickets)

The loss of autonomy:

I used to travel. I've been places. Had adventures. Explored.

Now my body and my bank account have decided: no more travel.

Not "travel less" or "travel differently." Just... no.

This section might as well not exist for me. It's written for people with resources and capability. I have neither.

Selecting destinations that cater to your interests and physical capabilities is crucial. Research destinations that are not only appealing but also age-friendly, with easy access to medical facilities, comfortable accommodations, and convenient transportation options. Cities with robust public transportation and a reputation for safety can be more relaxing and enjoyable, allowing you to focus on the experience rather than logistics.

Understanding healthcare options abroad is equally vital. Before traveling, investigate the healthcare services available at your chosen destination. This might mean looking into nearby hospitals or clinics that offer services comparable to those you might need at home. Additionally, familiarize yourself with the location's emergency services and keep a list of contact numbers handy in case of a medical emergency. It's also wise to consult your healthcare provider before traveling to discuss health considerations and any necessary vaccinations, which are crucial for protecting against potential health risks associated with certain destinations.

Travel insurance is an indispensable component of travel preparations, particularly for older adults. Comprehensive travel insurance that covers medical emergencies, trip cancellations, and lost luggage can provide peace of mind. When selecting a policy, ensure it covers pre-existing conditions and includes adequate medical evacuation coverage, which can be crucial if you require medical care that's best handled in your home country. Read the fine print and understand the extent of the coverage to avoid surprises during your travels.

Every sentence assumes you have money to spend on travel.

Healthcare abroad. Travel insurance. Medical evacuation coverage.

These are problems for people who CAN travel. I can't. Problem solved by poverty and disability.

Packing effectively can significantly enhance your travel experience, emphasizing comfort, health, and convenience. Start with a checklist of travel essentials that accommodate your specific needs. Comfortable clothing and footwear are a must, as they can make a significant difference in your daily outings and activities. Include medications in your original packaging, along with a copy of your prescriptions and a letter from your doctor detailing your medical needs. This preparation is essential for smooth travel through airport security and for obtaining necessary medications abroad if needed. Don't forget to pack any specialized health monitors or aids that support your daily health routines, ensuring you can maintain your wellness throughout your trip.

The grief of this section:

I'm not angry at the advice. It's good advice for people who can use it.

I'm grieving the life I don't get to have. The travel I can't do. The adventures that are permanently off-limits because of disability and poverty.

This isn't "aging optimization." This is "what you're missing because your body failed and you're poor."

Engaging safely with local cultures enriches your travel experience, offering more in-depth insights and more meaningful interactions. Partake in local activities that allow you to immerse yourself in the culture without compromising your safety or health. Food tours, museum visits, and guided city tours can be enjoyable ways to explore while providing structured, safe environments. Always listen to your body and respect your physical limits; schedule rest periods between activities to prevent exhaustion and maximize your enjoyment. When participating in any activity, whether it's a scenic hike or a cultural festival, always ensure you have clear information about the accessibility and physical demands, and don't hesitate to opt for lighter, more manageable experiences if necessary.

By carefully planning your travels, focusing on comfort and safety, and choosing activities that respect your physical capabilities, you can continue to explore the world with confidence and joy. This proactive approach to travel enhances your experiences and ensures that you remain healthy and vibrant, ready to enjoy each new adventure to the fullest.

6.5 Fashion and Personal Style in Your 40s and Beyond

In the colorful tapestry of life, the threads of fashion and personal style remain consistently intertwined with our identity and self-expression. As you navigate your 40s and beyond, these threads can evolve, reflecting changes in lifestyle, priorities, and physicality. Embracing this evolution in your attire by prioritizing comfort and accessibility doesn't mean sacrificing style; rather, it opens a new chapter of fashion that resonates with where you are in your life journey.

Adapting your wardrobe for comfort and accessibility becomes increasingly relevant as you age. This adaptation is not merely about opting for looser fits or softer fabrics but about finding clothing that simplifies your daily routine while enhancing your comfort. Adaptive clothing, designed with features such as magnetic buttons, velcro closures, and elasticated waistbands, can be particularly beneficial. These elements make dressing and undressing easier, especially for those dealing with reduced mobility or conditions like arthritis. However, the utility of these garments does not preclude style---many contemporary brands now offer adaptive clothing that is as trendy as it is functional. For instance, jeans with no-zip slip-on designs can look just as chic as traditional ones and are significantly easier to manage.

Adaptive clothing costs MORE than regular clothing.

The magnetic buttons, special closures, and thoughtful design—all add to the price.

What I actually wear:

Whatever I already own that I can get on and off with one functional arm. Stretchy clothes. Button-ups I can manage. Nothing new unless something wears out completely.

Shopping for disability-friendly clothing on disability income is darkly ironic.

The clothing designed for people with my limitations costs more than I can afford because I have my limitations.

Maintaining a personal style that boosts your confidence is crucial at any age. Your clothing is a powerful tool for self-expression, and feeling good in what you wear can significantly impact your overall happiness and self-esteem. The key is to align your wardrobe with your current lifestyle and body changes while keeping your personal aesthetics in mind. If you find comfort in vibrant colors and bold patterns, incorporate them into your new, more comfortable wardrobe. Accessories like scarves, hats, and jewelry can also play pivotal roles in maintaining your style. They can add personal flair to any outfit without compromising comfort, allowing you to express your personality in subtle yet impactful ways.

"Personal style" becomes "whatever doesn't hurt to put on."

I used to care about fashion. Had a style. Enjoyed dressing well.

Now my criteria are:

1. Can I get it on with limited shoulder mobility?

2. Is it comfortable for chronic pain?

3. Do I already own it (can't afford new)?

Style is a distant fourth priority.

Loss of autonomy:

My body dictates my wardrobe. My finances limit my options. I don't get to choose based on aesthetics or self-expression.

Shopping smartly for clothing that suits your aging body is both an art and a science. As our bodies change, so too do our sizing and fit needs. It's important to have your measurements updated regularly and to know how different brands' sizing works, as this can vary significantly. Opt for stores that offer personal shopping assistants who can help you find garments that fit your current body shape comfortably and stylishly. Additionally, online shopping can be a practical approach, particularly with retailers that provide detailed size guides and flexible return policies. This method allows you to try clothes on at home and assess them at your leisure, ensuring they not only fit well but also integrate seamlessly into your existing wardrobe.

"Personal shopping assistants" at stores I can't afford to shop at.

I buy clothing maybe once a year. Thrift stores if possible. Clearance racks. Whatever I can afford when something wears out.

There's no "shopping smartly for my aging body." There's "making do with what I can afford."

Incorporating age-appropriate trends into your wardrobe allows you to stay contemporary without feeling out of place. The fashion industry increasingly recognizes the diversity of ages in its clientele, offering styles that cater to a broad age range while still capturing current trends. For example, a well-tailored blazer or a classic trench coat can offer timeless elegance that is always in fashion. Pair these with trendier items like a statement piece of jewelry or a fashionable handbag to keep your look updated and vibrant. Remember, the goal is to blend comfort with style, ensuring that your fashion choices reflect your age, comfort needs, and personal taste seamlessly.

Well-tailored blazers and classic trench coats cost money I don't have.

Statement jewelry. Fashionable handbags. All assume disposable income for non-essentials.

What I have:

The clothes I owned before my disability. Wearing them until they fall apart. No "trends." No "contemporary style." Just... making my existing wardrobe last as long as possible.

Navigating the evolving landscape of fashion in your 40s and beyond offers an exciting opportunity to redefine your style, ensuring it aligns with your current lifestyle and comfort needs while still expressing who you are. By adapting your fashion choices, maintaining your personal style, shopping smartly, and thoughtfully incorporating contemporary trends, you create a wardrobe that looks great and feels great, enhancing your life with every outfit.

As this chapter closes, I want to acknowledge what the research consistently overlooks:

Lifestyle adjustments for "age optimization" assume you have resources.

Money for home modifications. Money for technology. Money for travel. Money for adaptive clothing. Money for decluttering services. Money for safety equipment.

What if you don't have money?

Then "lifestyle optimization" becomes "making do with what you have while watching your safety, comfort, and quality of life deteriorate because you can't afford solutions."

This isn't about being negative. This is about being honest:

Financial vulnerability and loss of autonomy aren't separate from aging—for many of us, they ARE the aging experience.

My body took away my autonomy over physical capabilities.

My disability took away my autonomy over my career and income.

My finances take away my autonomy over implementing solutions that might help.

The fear of financial vulnerability is rational when you're one emergency away from crisis.

The fear of losing autonomy is rational when every aspect of your life is controlled by factors outside your control—body, finances, systems not designed for people like you.

What I've learned:

Accept the limitations: I can't implement most "optimization" strategies. That's reality. Fighting reality is exhausting.

Use what's accessible: Free technology. Better lighting (affordable). Learning (free online). Connection (free video calls). I work with what I can access.

Grieve what's lost: I don't travel anymore. Can't afford home modifications. Can't optimize my wardrobe. These losses are real. Acknowledging them isn't a weakness.

Find autonomy where possible: I control my learning. My writing. My choices within my constraints. Small autonomy is still autonomy.

Prepare for crisis: An emergency fund is impossible, but I try. Know which bills can be delayed if needed. Have crisis plans. Financial vulnerability requires crisis thinking.

Disabled, poor, and largely powerless over my own circumstances, I've had to redefine "optimization."

It's not about ideal solutions. It's about surviving with dignity within brutal constraints.

That's not the chapter anyone wants to read. But it's the chapter some of us are living in.

And pretending otherwise doesn't help us. It just makes us invisible while we struggle.

Chapter 7: The Financial Cost Nobody Warns You About

I'm 58 years old, and I'm looking at taking out a second mortgage on my house for about $150,000.

Let me be clear: I'm not a financial advisor. I'm not going to tell you how to build a nest egg or maximize your 401(k). I'm drowning in debt myself, and a significant portion of that debt traces directly back to the cumulative injuries I sustained in my 20s, 30s, and 40s—the injuries this entire book has been about.

What I CAN tell you is this: when you're young and pushing through pain, when you're doing one more rep or running one more mile on an injured joint, you're not just damaging your body. You're setting up financial consequences that will compound for decades.

Nobody told me this when I was 25. Nobody sat me down and said, "Every time you ignore that pain, you're adding to a bill that will come due when you're 50."

So that's what this chapter is: the financial reality of "no pain, no gain" that nobody warns you about. The costs that accumulate. The savings you won't have. The financial choices you'll face when your body can't do the work anymore.

This isn't advice. This is a warning.

7.1 The Real Cost of Injury: What Nobody Calculates

The Immediate Costs (That Never Stop)

When you get injured, you think about the immediate costs: the ER visit, the X-ray, maybe some physical therapy if you're lucky enough to have insurance that covers it. What you don't realize is that these "immediate" costs never actually stop—they just morph into different forms that follow you for decades.

Here's what my cumulative injuries have cost me, just in the categories I can track:

Medical expenses (ongoing):

- Orthopedic appointments (multiple specialists over the years)
- Physical therapy sessions (some covered by insurance, many not)
- Imaging: X-rays, MRIs, CT scans to track deterioration
- Medications: pain management, anti-inflammatories, muscle relaxants
- Medical equipment: braces, supports, ergonomic modifications
- The surgery that ended my IT career (and all the follow-up care)

But those are just the line items on medical bills. The real costs go deeper.

The Hidden Costs Nobody Mentions

Lost earning potential: When your body can't do the work anymore, your income options narrow. I had to leave a lucrative IT career because I physically couldn't do the work. That's not just lost income—that's lost retirement contributions, lost career advancement, lost years of building toward financial security.

Reduced work hours: Even before I had to leave entirely, there were years when I couldn't work full-time. Couldn't sit at a desk for eight hours. Couldn't travel for work. Each reduction in hours was a reduction in income, in savings, in building toward a future that wouldn't be defined by financial stress.

Career changes forced by physical limitations: Sometimes you have to take a lower-paying job because it's all your body can handle. The financial impact of that compounds over the years.

Adaptive equipment and home modifications: That ergonomic desk chair? $800. The standing desk converter? $400. The modifications to your car so you can drive without pain? Another few hundred. None of this is covered by insurance. All of it is necessary.

The retirement savings you DON'T have: This is the big one. Every dollar that went to medical expenses and adaptive equipment was a dollar that didn't go into retirement savings. Every year of reduced income was a year of reduced contributions. The compound interest you lose over decades is staggering.

What "Prioritizing Health Expenditures" Actually Means

The original version of this chapter talked about "prioritizing health expenditures" and "investing in your longevity" as though these were optional choices you make with discretionary income.

Here's the reality: when you're dealing with cumulative injury, health expenditures aren't investments you choose to make. They're bills that come due whether you can afford them or not.

You don't "invest" in physical therapy. You need physical therapy or you can't function.

You don't "prioritize" pain management. You manage pain or you can't work.

You don't "budget for" orthopedic appointments. You go to orthopedic appointments or your condition worsens.

The language of "investment" implies choice and future returns. The reality of injury-related healthcare is that you're paying for damage already done, trying to maintain function you've already lost, managing a body that's already broken.

And yes, preventive care matters. Yes, regular check-ups can catch things early. But when you're young and invincible, pushing through pain because that's what athletes do, you're not thinking about preventive care. You're thinking about the next workout, the next fitness test, the next challenge to overcome.

By the time you realize you should have been "investing in your health," the damage is done and you're paying for repairs, not prevention.

What I Wish I'd Known at 25

If I could go back and tell my 25-year-old self one thing about the financial impact of injury, it would be this:

Every time you push through pain, you're taking out a loan against your future body—and the interest rate is brutal.

That knee you keep running on? That's going to cost you tens of thousands of dollars in medical care over the next thirty years, plus the income you'll lose when you can't do physical work anymore.

That back you keep straining? That's going to limit your career options in your 40s and cost you a six-figure income difference over your lifetime.

Those shoulders you keep pushing past their limits? That's going to require surgery that will put you out of work and drain your savings.

The financial cost of "no pain, no gain" isn't just the immediate medical bills. It's the compound effect of reduced earning potential, ongoing medical expenses, and the retirement savings you never built because you're too busy paying for the damage you did decades ago.

Financial Tools That Might Help (If You're Starting Now)

The original version of this chapter talked about FSAs and HSAs—Flexible Spending Accounts and Health Savings Accounts. These are real tools that can help with healthcare costs, and if you're young and reading this, they're worth understanding.

FSAs let you set aside pre-tax money for medical expenses, but you have to use it within the plan year. HSAs are available if you have a high-deductible health plan, and the money rolls over year to year.

Here's what I wish someone had told me about these:

1. If your employer offers an FSA, use it. Even if you're healthy now, you'll have medical expenses. Getting a tax break on them is better than nothing.

2. If you can afford a high-deductible health plan and qualify for an HSA, it's one of the few tax-advantaged ways to save for future medical costs. The money grows tax-free and you can withdraw it tax-free for medical expenses.

3. If you're dealing with cumulative injury like I am, you'll blow through your FSA contribution every year. It helps, but it doesn't come close to covering the actual costs.

4. HSAs are great in theory, but only if you can afford to contribute to them while also covering your current medical expenses. If you're living paycheck to paycheck because of medical bills, you're not building HSA savings.

The reality is that these tools help at the margins. They make healthcare costs slightly more manageable. But they don't change the fundamental equation: injury is expensive, and that expense compounds over decades.

Apps and Budgeting Tools: Tracking the Damage

Yes, apps like Mint or YNAB can help you track healthcare spending. I've used them. They're useful for seeing where your money goes.

What they can't do is change the fact that healthcare expenses aren't really optional or flexible. When the app tells you you've spent $500 this month on medical costs and you've blown your budget, you don't have the option to just... stop having medical costs.

The app shows you the reality. It doesn't fix it.

But if you're young and reading this, here's what tracking can do for you: it can show you the PATTERN before it becomes overwhelming. If you're seeing increasing medical costs from sports injuries or pushing too hard at the gym, that's data. That's information you can use to make different choices before the damage compounds.

Cost vs. Benefit: When You're Already Paying for Past Mistakes

The original chapter talked about evaluating cost versus benefit for treatments. This makes sense in theory.

In practice, when you're dealing with cumulative injury, the "benefit" is often just maintaining current function or preventing further deterioration. You're not making choices between "good" and "better." You're making choices between "bad" and "worse."

Should you pay for that physical therapy session that insurance won't cover? Well, if you don't, your range of motion will decrease further and you'll need more invasive treatment later. So yes, you pay for it, even though you can't really afford it.

Should you get that MRI to see how much the deterioration has progressed? Well, if you don't, you won't know how to modify your activities to prevent further damage. So yes, you get it, even though it costs $800 out of pocket.

These aren't "investments in longevity." These are damage control expenses.

The Financial Reality I'm Living

I'm looking at a second mortgage because decades of medical expenses and reduced earning potential have left me without the retirement savings I should have built. The damage I did to my body in my 20s and 30s is still costing me money in my late 50s—and it will continue costing me money for the rest of my life.

This isn't a success story about smart financial planning. This is a cautionary tale about the long-term financial consequences of "no pain, no gain."

If you're young and you're reading this, please understand: the pain you're pushing through today has a price tag. And you'll be paying it for decades.

7.2 Insurance Reality: What Actually Gets Covered (And What Doesn't)

The Insurance You Think You Have vs. The Coverage You Actually Have

When I was in the Air Force, I had military healthcare. When I worked in IT, I had employer-provided insurance. I thought I was covered. I thought insurance meant my medical expenses would be handled.

Here's what I learned: insurance covers some things. The things it doesn't cover are often the things you need most when dealing with cumulative injury.

What insurance typically DOES cover:
- Emergency care (when something acute happens)
- Doctor visits (with co-pays)
- Some physical therapy (usually limited sessions)
- Medications (if they're on the formulary)
- Surgery (if deemed "medically necessary")

What insurance typically DOESN'T cover:
- Ongoing physical therapy beyond the approved number of sessions
- Ergonomic equipment and adaptive devices
- Alternative treatments that might help but aren't "standard care"
- Preventive care that goes beyond annual check-ups
- The full cost of specialists (hello, co-pays and deductibles)
- Time off work for recovery

That gap between "covered" and "not covered" is where you'll spend thousands of dollars out of pocket.

Understanding Your Insurance (Before You Need It)

The original version of this chapter explained Medicare parts A, B, C, and D. That information is accurate and you can find it anywhere. What they don't tell you is this:

By the time you're eligible for Medicare at 65, you've already spent decades paying out of pocket for the things insurance didn't cover. Medicare helps with future costs, but it doesn't reimburse you for the thirty years of expenses you've already incurred.

If you're younger and reading this, here's what actually matters about your current insurance:

1. Know your deductible. This is how much you pay out of pocket before insurance kicks in. If you have a $5,000 deductible and you're dealing with ongoing injury care, you'll hit that every single year.

2. Know your out-of-pocket maximum. This is the most you'll pay in a year before insurance covers 100%. When you're dealing with cumulative injury, you'll hit this too.

3. Know what counts toward those limits. Some plans don't count co-pays toward your out-of-pocket max. Some don't count out-of-network care. Read the fine print.

4. Understand "medical necessity." Insurance will deny coverage for treatments they don't deem medically necessary, even if your doctor recommends them. You'll either go without or pay out of pocket.

The Insurance Battles You'll Fight

Here's what they don't tell you: having insurance doesn't mean you won't fight with insurance companies.

I've had insurance deny coverage for:
- Physical therapy sessions beyond their arbitrary limit (even though my condition required ongoing care)
- MRIs to track deterioration (they wanted to wait until it was "worse"—which means more damage)
- Medications that weren't on their preferred list (even though the alternatives didn't work for me)
- Specialist referrals (because the primary care doctor should be able to handle it, according to them)

Each denial meant either paying out of pocket or going without care. Each appeal took time and energy I didn't have while dealing with chronic pain and limited function.

This is the reality of insurance when you're dealing with long-term injury consequences.

Long-Term Care: The Thing Nobody Wants to Think About

The original chapter talked about long-term care insurance and when to buy it. Here's the reality:

Long-term care insurance is expensive. If you're already struggling with medical expenses from cumulative injury, you probably can't afford it. And if you already have significant health issues, you might not qualify for it at all.

But here's what you need to know: cumulative injury increases your likelihood of needing long-term care earlier than expected. When your body is broken down by your 50s, you might need assisted living or in-home care in your 60s or 70s rather than your 80s or 90s.

This is another financial cost of "no pain, no gain" that nobody calculates when they're young.

If you CAN afford long-term care insurance in your 50s, and if you qualify, it might be worth it. But most people dealing with the financial aftermath of decades of injury can't afford it—which means you'll be paying for long-term care out of pocket when you need it, further depleting whatever savings you have left.

What I Wish I'd Done Differently

If I could go back, here's what I would have done regarding insurance:

1. Actually read my insurance policies when I was young and healthy, so I understood what was and wasn't covered before I needed it.

2. Used every bit of preventive care that WAS covered—the annual physicals, the screenings, the check-ups—to catch problems before they compounded.

3. Fought harder with insurance companies when they denied coverage for things I needed, instead of just accepting the denials and going without care.

4. Saved money specifically for healthcare costs, knowing that insurance wouldn't cover everything.

But mostly, I wish I hadn't damaged my body in the first place. Because no amount of insurance preparation can change the fact that cumulative injury is expensive, and much of that expense falls on you regardless of your coverage.

Healthcare Directives: The Legal Side

The original chapter talked about advanced directives and powers of attorney. This is actually important, and it's something I HAVE done correctly.

Advanced healthcare directives specify your medical treatment preferences if you become incapacitated. A durable power of attorney for healthcare designates someone to make medical decisions if you can't.

When you're dealing with cumulative injury and ongoing health issues, these documents are even more critical. You've already experienced the medical system. You know what treatments you would and wouldn't want. You know who you trust to make decisions for you.

Getting these documents in place isn't expensive (you can often do it through legal aid or online services), and it provides massive peace of mind. This is one area of financial planning where a small upfront cost prevents huge problems later.

Do this. Regardless of your age or current health status, do this. It's one of the few proactive financial decisions that doesn't require ongoing expense.

7.3 Retirement Planning: When There's Nothing to Plan With

The Retirement You're Supposed to Have vs. The One You Actually Get

The original version of this chapter talked about calculating retirement needs using the "80% rule"—the idea that you'll need about 80% of your pre-retirement salary to maintain your lifestyle in retirement.

Here's what that assumes:

- That you had a consistent salary to base that percentage on
- That you weren't forced to reduce work hours or change careers due to physical limitations
- That you were able to save consistently throughout your working years
- Those medical expenses didn't consume what should have been retirement savings
- That you're retiring by choice at a planned age, not because your body gave out

When cumulative injury derails your career and drains your finances, none of those assumptions hold.

The Reality of "Retirement" When Your Body Quits First

I didn't retire from IT. My body made it impossible to continue working in IT, and I had to find other work I could physically manage. That's not retirement planning—that's crisis management.

When your body forces career changes or early exit from the workforce, "retirement planning" becomes "figuring out how to survive financially with limited options."

The retirement calculators ask: "How much do you need to save to maintain your desired lifestyle?"

The reality asks: "How will you pay your bills when you can't work anymore?"

These are very different questions.

What "Building a Nest Egg" Actually Requires

The original chapter talked about diversifying investments, maximizing 401(k) contributions, and building a balanced portfolio. All sound advice—if you have money to invest.

Here's what it takes to build retirement savings:
- Consistent income (hard when injury forces reduced hours or career changes)
- Money left over after expenses (hard when medical costs are ongoing)
- Decades of compound growth (hard when you have to withdraw from savings for medical emergencies)
- Employer matching on 401(k) (only works if you're employed full-time, which physical limitations might prevent)

I know the theory. I understand compound interest and investment diversification. What I didn't have was the consistent financial stability to apply any of it, because I was too busy paying for the medical consequences of damage I'd done decades earlier.

The Retirement Savings You DON'T Have: A Case Study

Let me break down what "no retirement savings" actually looks like in real numbers:

If I had been able to work full-time in IT from age 25 to 65, contributing just 10% of my salary to a 401(k) with employer matching, and assuming modest 7% annual returns, I would have accumulated somewhere around $800,000 to $1 million by retirement age.

Instead, here's what actually happened:

- Career reduced to part-time due to physical limitations: Lost years of contributions
- Career ended entirely in my 40s: Lost decades of compound growth
- Had to withdraw from what little savings I had for medical expenses: Lost principal and future growth
- Medical debt accumulated: No ability to save new money
- Current retirement savings: Virtually nothing

The difference between what my retirement SHOULD look like and what it ACTUALLY looks like is somewhere around $1 million. That's the financial cost of cumulative injury compounded over decades.

This isn't meant to depress you. It's meant to show you that the financial consequences of "no pain, no gain" are real, quantifiable, and devastating.

What Young People Need to Understand About Retirement

If you're in your 20s or 30s reading this, retirement seems impossibly far away. You can't imagine being 65. The idea of saving for something 40 years in the future feels abstract.

Here's what you need to understand: Time is the most powerful factor in retirement savings, and you can't get it back.

Every year you work and contribute to retirement accounts is a year in which money grows. Every year you DON'T contribute because you're paying for medical costs or can't work due to injury is a year of lost growth that you can never recover.

The 25-year-old who contributes $5,000 a year for 40 years will end up with more than the 45-year-old who contributes $15,000 a year for 20 years, even though the total contributed is the same. That's the power of compound growth over time.

When cumulative injury steals your working years, it steals your retirement savings. Not just the contributions you would have made, but all the growth those contributions would have generated.

This is why "no pain, no gain" is so financially catastrophic. You're not just paying medical bills. You're losing the single most valuable asset you have for retirement: time.

Retirement Accounts: Use Them If You Can

Despite my own financial reality, I still believe in the value of retirement accounts IF you have the ability to use them:

401(k)s with employer matching: This is free money. If your employer offers matching and you can afford to contribute, do it. Even if you can only contribute enough to get the full match, do it.

IRAs (Individual Retirement Accounts): These offer tax advantages for retirement savings. Traditional IRAs give you a tax break now; Roth IRAs are taxed now but are tax-free in retirement. If you have money to save, use these vehicles.

The problem is that "if you have money to save" is a big if when you're dealing with medical expenses from cumulative injury.

But if you're young and you DON'T have those expenses yet, use every retirement savings tool available to you. Build that cushion now, while you can, because you might not always have the ability to do so.

Adjusting Your "Plan" When There Was No Plan to Begin With

The original chapter talked about regularly reviewing and adjusting your retirement plan to accommodate life changes.

When there's no retirement plan—when you're just trying to survive financially from month to month—there's nothing to adjust.

What there IS is a constant recalculation of: "How long can I keep working? What work can my body still do? How will I pay bills when I can't work anymore?"

This is the retirement "planning" of someone living with the financial consequences of cumulative injury.

If you're in this position too, here's what I can tell you:

- Social Security will provide something, but it won't be enough to live on comfortably
- You'll probably need to work longer than you want to, in whatever capacity your body allows
- You'll need to be creative about reducing expenses and finding income sources that don't require physical capacity
- You'll need to accept that your retirement won't look like the magazine photos of couples on beaches

It's not the retirement anyone dreams of. But it's survivable.

The Professional Advice I Can't Afford

The original chapter recommended consulting financial advisors to optimize retirement planning. This is good advice if you have assets to optimize.

When you don't have assets—when you have debt and medical expenses and no savings—financial advisors can't create money out of thin air. They can help you manage what you have, but they can't solve the fundamental problem of "no money to manage."

If you DO have some assets and you're trying to make the most of limited resources, a financial advisor might help you prioritize and strategize. But understand that their advice will be constrained by your reality.

What I can tell you without needing a financial advisor: Start saving for retirement as early as possible. Use every tax-advantaged account available. Don't assume your body will let you work until 65. And don't destroy your body chasing fitness goals that will cost you your financial future.

That last one? That's the advice worth more than anything a financial professional could tell you.

7.4 Legal Planning: Protecting What Little You Have

Why Legal Planning Matters Even When You Have Nothing

When you hear "estate planning," you probably think of wealthy people with assets to distribute. Wills and trusts sound like things you need when you have money.

Here's the reality: legal planning matters even more when you DON'T have money, because you can't afford the legal complications that arise without it.

When you have limited assets, every dollar counts. Proper legal planning ensures that what little you have goes where you want it to go, without being consumed by legal fees and probate costs.

Wills: The Minimum You Must Do

A will is a legal document that specifies how your assets should be distributed after you die. Even if your "assets" are minimal—a car, some personal belongings, maybe a house with a mortgage—you need a will.

Without a will, the state decides who gets what according to intestacy laws. This might not match your wishes. It will definitely involve legal processes that cost money and take time, depleting what little estate you have.

A basic will isn't expensive. You can create one through online legal services for under $100, or through legal aid if you qualify. There is no excuse not to have one.

What should be in your will:
- Who gets your possessions (be specific about items with sentimental value)
- Who you want to handle your estate (your executor)
- If you have minor children, who should be their guardian
- Any specific instructions about your wishes

Update your will when major life events happen: marriage, divorce, births, and deaths. Keep it current.

Trusts: Probably Not Necessary If You're Like Me

The original chapter talked extensively about revocable and irrevocable trusts. These are useful tools for people with significant assets who want control over how those assets are distributed or want to minimize estate taxes.

If you're dealing with debt and limited assets, trusts are probably overkill. The legal costs of setting up and maintaining a trust likely exceed any benefit you'd get from having one.

That said, there are specific situations where even people with modest means might benefit from a trust:
- If you have a special needs family member who might lose government benefits if they inherit directly
- If you have minor children and want to control how assets are distributed to them over time
- If you own property and want to avoid probate

But for most people in financial situations like mine, a simple will is sufficient.

Advanced Directives: THIS Is Critical

Advanced healthcare directives are legal documents that specify your medical treatment preferences if you become unable to communicate. This is separate from a will—it's about medical decisions while you're alive, not asset distribution after you die.

When you're dealing with chronic health issues from cumulative injury, advanced directives are absolutely essential.

What you need:

Living Will (Advanced Healthcare Directive): This document specifies what medical treatments you do and don't want in specific situations. Do you want to be kept on life support if there's no chance of recovery? Do you want aggressive treatment or comfort care? What are your wishes about resuscitation?

These are hard questions. Answer them anyway, and put the answers in writing.

Durable Power of Attorney for Healthcare: This designates someone to make medical decisions on your behalf if you can't make them yourself. Choose someone who knows your values, who will respect your wishes even under pressure, and who can handle the stress of medical decision-making.

This is not the same as your executor (the person who handles your will). This is about medical decisions while you're alive.

Durable Power of Attorney for Finances: This designates someone to handle your financial affairs if you're incapacitated. Pay your bills, manage your accounts, deal with insurance—all the financial tasks you can't do yourself.

Why This Matters When You Have Limited Assets

You might think, "I don't have money, so why do I need someone to manage my finances if I'm incapacitated?"

Because bills don't stop coming just because you're in the hospital. Your mortgage or rent still needs to be paid. Insurance claims still need to be filed. Bank accounts still need to be managed.

Without a durable power of attorney for finances, your family would need to go to court to get the authority to handle these things for you. That costs money you don't have and takes time you don't have.

Setting up a durable power of attorney is simple and inexpensive. Do it.

How to Set These Documents Up

You don't need an expensive attorney to create basic legal documents. Options include:

Online legal services: Sites like LegalZoom or Nolo offer document templates for under $100. They walk you through the questions and generate the legal documents.

Legal aid: If you have limited income, you might qualify for free legal assistance through legal aid organizations. They can help you create wills, advanced directives, and powers of attorney.

State-specific forms: Many states provide free advanced directive forms through their Department of Health or Aging and Disability Services. These are legally valid and cost nothing.

DIY with witnesses: In some states, you can create legal documents yourself as long as they're properly witnessed and notarized. Check your state's requirements.

What you SHOULD spend money on: Having an attorney review your documents to make sure they're valid and complete. This might cost $200-500, but it's worth it to ensure everything is correct.

Keeping Documents Updated

Life changes. Your wishes change. Your designated decision-makers might become unavailable. Your financial situation changes.

Review your legal documents every 3-5 years, and immediately after major life events:
- Marriage or divorce
- Birth or adoption of children
- Death of your designated executor or power of attorney
- Major health changes
- Significant financial changes

Updating is usually simpler and cheaper than creating new documents from scratch.

Where to Keep These Documents

Legal documents don't help if nobody can find them when needed.

Keep originals in a safe place (fireproof safe, safety deposit box) and give copies to:
- Your designated executor
- Your designated power of attorney for healthcare
- Your designated power of attorney for finances
- Your primary care doctor (copy of healthcare directives)
- A trusted family member

Make sure the people who need these documents know where to find them.

The One Area of Legal Planning I Got Right

Despite my financial struggles, I have done this part correctly. I have:

- A current will specifying how my assets (such as they are) should be distributed
- Advanced healthcare directives specifying my medical treatment preferences
- Designated powers of attorney for both healthcare and finances
- Copies distributed to the appropriate people
- Documents reviewed and updated after major life changes

This gives me peace of mind that, even though I don't have the financial security I wish I had, at least my wishes will be respected and my loved ones won't face legal complications on top of everything else.

This is the one area of financial planning that doesn't require wealth. It requires only forethought and a few hundred dollars. There is no excuse not to do it.

Protecting What Matters

Legal planning isn't just about money and assets. It's about ensuring that your wishes are respected, that your loved ones aren't burdened with legal complications, and that you maintain some control over your medical care and financial affairs even when you can't speak for yourself.

When you don't have much financially, protecting what you DO have becomes even more critical. These legal documents are how you do that.

7.5 The Economics of Aging with a Broken Body

Adjusting Spending When You Have No Choice

The original chapter talked about "adjusting spending habits with age" as though this is a voluntary optimization—cutting unnecessary subscriptions, downsizing your home, switching to a more fuel-efficient car.

Here's the reality when cumulative injury has destroyed your finances: you're not optimizing spending. You're in survival mode.

Spending adjustments when you're in debt and have limited income:

- You're not downsizing to "allocate more toward retirement savings." You're downsizing because you can't afford your current housing.
- You're not cutting subscriptions to "maximize income." You're cutting everything non-essential because you need that money for medical expenses and basic bills.
- You're not choosing a fuel-efficient car. You're driving whatever car you have until it dies because you can't afford to replace it.

This isn't financial planning. This is financial triage.

If you're reading this and you're young, understand: this is what "adjusting spending with age" actually looks like when decades of medical expenses have consumed your income. It's not a choice. It's a necessity.

The Debt You Can't Escape

The original chapter recommended tackling high-interest debt using the "avalanche approach"—paying off the highest-interest debts first to minimize interest paid over time.

This is sound advice if you have the income to implement it.

When you're dealing with the financial aftermath of cumulative injury, here's the reality:

- You're often in survival mode, paying minimums on everything and hoping nothing breaks

- Medical debt keeps accumulating, faster than you can pay down existing debt
- "Prioritizing" which debt to pay first is a luxury when you barely have enough to cover minimums
- Debt consolidation might lower your interest rate, but it doesn't reduce the total you owe

I'm not saying don't try to reduce debt. I'm saying that when injury has decimated your earning potential and medical expenses continue, debt reduction is aspirational more than achievable.

The goal becomes: don't let debt get worse. Don't default. Don't destroy your credit entirely. Survive.

If you can do more than that—if you can actually pay down debt—then yes, focus on high-interest debt first. But if you're just trying to keep your head above water, know that you're not alone.

Investing in Your Senior Years: What a Joke

The original chapter talked about "low-risk investments that provide stable and reliable income" in your senior years. Bonds. Dividend-paying stocks. Real estate investment trusts.

Let me be blunt: if you don't have money to invest, advice about investment strategies is meaningless.

When you're 58 and looking at a second mortgage just to cover existing debt and medical expenses, "investing" is not on the table. There is no investment portfolio to diversify. There are no dividend-paying stocks generating passive income. There is no careful balance of risk and return.

There is only: "How do I pay my bills this month?"

If you're young and you DO have the ability to invest—if you have income beyond expenses, if you're building retirement accounts, if you have money that isn't immediately needed for survival—then yes, learn about investing. Diversify. Build that portfolio.

But understand that cumulative injury can take all of that away. The investment strategy you build in your 30s can be completely destroyed by medical expenses and lost income in your 40s and 50s.

I'm not telling you this to discourage you from investing. I'm telling you this so you understand the stakes. Your health IS your wealth. Protect it.

Financial Scams: Adding Insult to Injury

The original chapter warned about financial scams targeting older adults. This is real and important.

When you're financially desperate, you become more vulnerable to scams that promise quick money or debt relief. When you're dealing with chronic pain and limited cognitive bandwidth, you're more vulnerable to manipulation.

Common financial scams targeting people in difficult financial situations:

- "Debt relief" services that charge fees and don't actually reduce your debt
- Predatory loans with astronomical interest rates disguised as helpful options
- Investment schemes promising guaranteed returns (nothing is guaranteed)
- Medical discount programs that cost more than they save
- Reverse mortgage schemes that strip equity from your home

The best protection against financial scams: skepticism. If it sounds too good to be true, it is. If someone is pressuring you to act immediately, walk away. If they're asking for money upfront, it's probably a scam.

Get advice from someone you trust before making any major financial decision. When you're desperate, your judgment is compromised. That's when scammers strike.

What I Wish I Could Tell You About the "Economics of Aging"

I wish I could tell you that if you plan carefully, you'll be financially secure in your senior years. I wish I could tell you that smart budgeting and wise investments guarantee a comfortable retirement.

I can't tell you that, because it's not true.

What I CAN tell you is this:
- The choices you make about your body in your 20s and 30s will have financial consequences for the rest of your life
- Cumulative injury doesn't just cost you money—it costs you earning potential, career options, and retirement security
- Medical expenses from long-term injury are ongoing and often not fully covered by insurance
- Building financial security requires both income and health, and you might not always have both
- The time to protect your financial future is NOW, while you still have the health and earning capacity to do so

The economics of aging with a broken body is brutal. Every financial planning strategy assumes you'll have consistent income and manageable expenses. Cumulative injury destroys both of those assumptions.

Chapter Conclusion: The Bill Comes Due

I opened this chapter by telling you I'm looking at a second mortgage for $150,000 This isn't because I made bad financial decisions in the traditional sense—I didn't gamble, didn't overspend on luxuries, didn't live beyond my means.

This is the compounded financial cost of decades of cumulative injury that started when I was in my 20s, pushing through pain because "no pain, no gain."

The bill for those injuries has been coming due for thirty years:

- In medical expenses that consumed what should have been savings
- In reduced earning potential when my body couldn't do the work
- In career changes forced by physical limitations
- In the retirement accounts I never built
- In the debt I accumulated just to survive

And the bill is STILL coming due. It will continue coming due for the rest of my life.

This chapter wasn't the financial planning guide I originally wrote. It's a financial warning.

If you're young, if you're still healthy, if you're still pushing through pain to achieve fitness goals or prove your toughness: understand that you're not just risking your body. You're risking your financial future.

The workout that damages your knee today will cost you tens of thousands of dollars over the next thirty years.

The injury you ignore now will limit your career options later.

The "no pain, no gain" mentality will leave you with plenty of pain and nothing gained except debt and disability.

I can't tell you how to build wealth. I can only tell you how easily cumulative injury can destroy it.

The most valuable financial advice I can give you: Protect your body. It's the foundation of everything else. Without your health, no amount of financial planning will save you.

That's the economics of aging that nobody tells you about.

Chapter 8 Overcoming Age-Related Challenges

Have you ever wondered why, as the years stack up, your body starts to signal in ways it never did before? It's like gaining a new sense, but instead of superhero abilities, you're noticing fluctuations in mood, weight, and even your desire for intimacy. These aren't just random occurrences; they're tied to the ebb and flow of hormones within your body, a natural aspect of aging that affects everyone, though not uniformly. In this chapter, we'll unwrap the layers of hormonal changes that accompany aging, providing you with the insights and tools necessary to manage and optimize your well-being during these transformative years.

8.1 Handling Hormonal Changes and Their Impacts

Understanding Hormonal Changes

Hormones, the body's chemical messengers, orchestrate a range of physiological functions, from growth and metabolism to mood and reproductive health. As you age, these hormone levels, particularly reproductive hormones like estrogen and testosterone, naturally decline, a process that can start as early as your 30s and continue throughout your life. This hormonal shift isn't just about fertility; it impacts a wide range of bodily systems and can significantly influence your physical health, emotional well-being, and overall quality of life.

Estrogen and testosterone decreasecan affect your metabolic rate, bone density, muscle strength, and fat distribution. This shift can lead to noticeable changes in your body shape and how efficiently you burn calories. Moreover, these hormones also influence skin elasticity and hydration, which is why changes in their levels can accelerate the appearance of aging skin. Understanding these changes is crucial not only for your physical health but for setting realistic expectations about what aging means for your body.

Symptoms and Signs

Navigating through this hormonal transition, you might experience a variety of symptoms that, at first glance, might seem unrelated. Women may notice hot flashes, night sweats, mood swings, and changes in menstrual patterns as early signs of perimenopause leading into menopause. Men, though often less discussed, undergo a comparable transition known as andropause, which can manifest as fatigue, depression, reduced libido, and difficulty achieving or maintaining an erection.

Identifying these symptoms early on is crucial for effective management. However, because these signs can vary widely in both type and severity, understanding your own body's responses is key. Keeping a journal of your physical and emotional health can help you and your healthcare provider recognize patterns and correlations with hormonal changes.

Management Strategies

Addressing hormonal changes involves a multi-faceted approach that includes lifestyle adjustments, dietary strategies, and possibly medical interventions. Regular physical activity, particularly strength training and cardiovascular exercises, can mitigate muscle loss, improve mood, and enhance metabolic rate. Nutrition also plays a critical role; for instance, foods rich in calcium and vitamin D are crucial for bone health, while balanced meals can help manage weight and energy levels.

For some, lifestyle changes alone might not suffice, and hormone replacement therapy (HRT) could be a viable option. HRT can alleviate many of the symptoms associated with hormonal decline, but it's not suitable for everyone. The decision to use HRT should be made in consultation with a healthcare provider, taking into account your personal health history and risk factors.

Monitoring and Testing

Keeping track of your hormonal health requires regular monitoring and testing, which can provide critical insights into your hormonal levels and help guide management strategies. Blood tests, saliva tests, and urine tests are among the common methods used to assess hormone levels. These tests can help determine if your symptoms are indeed linked to hormonal changes or if other underlying health issues may be contributing.

The frequency of these tests can vary depending on individual factors such as age, symptoms, and health history. Generally, it is advisable to undergo hormonal assessments at the onset of symptoms and periodically thereafter to monitor the effectiveness of any treatments or lifestyle adjustments. Your doctor can provide personalized recommendations on testing frequency and the best types of tests for your specific situation.

By understanding the biological underpinnings of hormonal changes, recognizing the associated symptoms, employing effective management strategies, and maintaining regular monitoring, you can navigate the challenges of hormonal fluctuations with greater ease and confidence. This proactive approach not only enhances your immediate quality of life but also sets a solid foundation for healthy aging, allowing you to embrace each year with vitality and positivity.

8.2 The Truth About Menopause and Andropause

Menopause and andropause represent significant, yet often misunderstood, stages in adult development, marking the conclusion of reproductive hormone production in women and men, respectively. Typically, menopause occurs in women between the ages of 45 and 55 when the ovaries cease producing estrogen and progesterone, signaling the end of menstrual cycles. Andropause, though less dramatic in onset, affects men usually after the age of 50, characterized by a gradual decline in testosterone levels, which can impact everything from muscle mass to mood regulation. Both of these physiological processes signify more than just the end of fertility; they reflect a broader shift in the hormonal balance that can influence numerous aspects of health and well-being.

Managing the symptoms associated with these transitions can significantly enhance quality of life. For many women, menopause brings hot flashes, night sweats, and insomnia, along with emotional disturbances such as irritability or sudden sadness. Men might not have hot flashes, but they often experience fatigue, mood changes, and changes in sexual function due to andropause. Effective management of these symptoms often starts with lifestyle modifications. Regular physical activity, for instance, can help mitigate weight gain and improve mood, while a balanced diet rich in calcium and vitamin D supports bone health, particularly crucial as hormonal changes can accelerate bone density loss. Keeping bedrooms cool and avoiding heavy meals or caffeine close to bedtime can also help reduce the severity of night sweats and improve sleep quality.

Beyond lifestyle tweaks, several therapeutic options are available to manage menopause and andropause symptoms. Hormone replacement therapy (HRT) is perhaps the most well-known treatment for menopause, involving medications that contain female hormones to replace the ones the body no longer makes post-menopause. This treatment can be highly effective in treating many of the symptoms of menopause, such as hot flashes and vaginal discomfort. However, HRT isn't suitable for everyone and carries some risks, such as an increased risk of blood clots and certain types of cancer. It's crucial to have a thorough discussion with a healthcare provider to understand the benefits and risks based on your personal health history. For men, testosterone replacement therapy can help alleviate symptoms of andropause, including low libido and fatigue, but, like HRT, it requires careful medical supervision due to potential risks like heart disease and prostate health issues.

Herbal supplements and natural therapies offer alternatives or a complement to hormone therapy. Phytoestrogens, plant-derived compounds found in soy products, have a chemical structure similar to that of human estrogen and can act as a mild form of estrogen replacement, helping to balance hormone levels naturally. Other herbal supplements like black cohosh for women and saw palmetto for men have been traditionally used to manage menopause and andropause symptoms, respectively. While these natural remedies can be beneficial, it's essential to consult a healthcare provider before starting any new supplement, especially if you are taking other medications or have underlying health conditions.

Addressing these hormonal changes comprehensively is not only about alleviating immediate discomfort but also about safeguarding long-term health. Women undergoing menopause experience a rapid decline in bone density, increasing their risk of osteoporosis. Ensuring adequate intake of calcium and vitamin D, along with regular weight-bearing exercise, can help maintain bone strength. Both men and women should also be mindful of their cardiovascular health, as changes in hormone levels during menopause and andropause can influence heart health. A heart-healthy diet rich in fruits, vegetables, whole grains, and lean proteins, along with regular cardiovascular exercise, plays a critical role in preventing heart disease. Additionally, regular check-ups and screenings become even more crucial during this period to monitor health changes and adjust care plans as necessary.

By embracing a proactive approach to managing menopause and andropause, you can navigate these transitions more smoothly and maintain a vibrant, healthy life in the years that follow. Whether through lifestyle modifications, therapeutic interventions, or a combination of both, the key is to stay informed and engaged with your health care providers, ensuring that your choices are tailored to your unique health needs and life circumstances.

8.3 Chronic Conditions: Prevention and Management Tips

As the years advance, so does the likelihood of encountering chronic conditions that can significantly impact the quality of your life. Common ailments such as diabetes, arthritis, and cardiovascular diseases are not just mere inconveniences; they are profound health challenges that can dictate the pace and enjoyment of your later years. However, the onset or exacerbation of these conditions can often be mitigated through informed lifestyle choices and proactive health management.

Diabetes, a metabolic disorder, that I have, characterized by high blood sugar levels, is increasingly prevalent among older adults. Similarly, arthritis, which causes pain and inflammation in the joints, commonly develops or worsens with age, significantly impairing mobility and daily comfort. Cardiovascular diseases, including hypertension and heart disease, are major health concerns that can lead to severe complications if not properly managed. The thread connecting these conditions is not just their prevalence but also the fact that lifestyle plays a crucial role in their management and prevention.

Preventing these conditions begins with embracing a lifestyle that supports overall bodily health. Regular physical activity is paramount; not only does it help regulate blood sugar levels, aiding in diabetes management, but it also improves cardiovascular health and can alleviate the symptoms of arthritis by strengthening the muscles around the joints. The type of activity does matter—low-impact exercises like swimming, cycling, or walking are often most suitable for older adults, as they deliver the necessary health benefits without unduly stressing the joints.

Diet, too, plays a critical role in preventing and managing these diseases. A balanced diet rich in fruits, vegetables, whole grains, and lean proteins can help manage weight, reduce blood pressure, and improve cholesterol levels, all of which are risk factors for diabetes and cardiovascular diseases. For joint health, foods rich in omega-3 fatty acids, such as salmon and flaxseeds, can reduce inflammation. Moreover, incorporating anti-inflammatory spices like turmeric and ginger into your diet can also provide relief from arthritis symptoms. Avoiding excessive sugar and salt intake is crucial, particularly for those managing diabetes or at risk of heart disease.

Besides lifestyle adjustments, effective management of chronic conditions often requires adherence to medical advice and prescribed treatments. Medications play a critical role and must be taken as directed by healthcare professionals. Regular check-ups allow for ongoing adjustments to your treatment plan as needed. It's also important to stay informed about your conditions and treatments. This can involve reading up on the latest research, discussing your condition with healthcare providers, and possibly attending workshops or classes that offer education on managing your specific health issues.

Utilizing healthcare resources is essential for effective disease management. Regular visits to your primary care physician or specialists like cardiologists or endocrinologists can help monitor the progression of your condition and the effectiveness of your treatment plan. For those with arthritis, working with a physical therapist can provide tailored exercises that improve joint function without exacerbating pain. Support groups and patient education programs offer a community of support and a wealth of information, helping you to feel empowered and less isolated in managing your condition.

Incorporating these preventive measures and management techniques into your daily routine requires commitment, but remember that the goal is to enhance your quality of life. By actively engaging in your health care, making informed lifestyle choices, and utilizing available resources, you can significantly influence the impact of chronic conditions, maintaining your vitality and independence for years to come. This proactive approach helps manage existing conditions and serves as a preventive measure against the development of additional health issues, allowing you to lead a fuller, more active life despite the challenges that may come with age.

8.4 Eyesight and Hearing: Protecting Your Senses

As we age, our senses—the windows through which we experience the world—naturally begin to dull. Our eyesight and hearing, in particular, tend to decline, a process usually gradual and often initially imperceptible. Understanding these changes is crucial not just for adapting to them but for taking proactive steps to mitigate their impact on our daily lives. Conditions such as presbyopia, cataracts, and age-related hearing loss are common as we grow older. Presbyopia, the inability to focus on close objects, typically starts in the early to mid-40s and is a natural part of the aging process of the eye. Cataracts, which cloud the lens of the eye and impair vision, develop slowly and usually later in life. Age-related hearing loss, meanwhile, can begin as early as one's 30s or 40s but is most common in those 60 and older, affecting the ability to hear higher frequencies at first and, over time, potentially all frequencies.

Preventative care plays a pivotal role in managing these age-related changes. For eyesight, protecting your eyes from UV light is crucial; prolonged exposure to sunlight can accelerate conditions like cataracts. Wearing sunglasses with UV protection or wide-brimmed hats when outdoors can significantly reduce this risk. Nutrition also plays a key role in eye health. A diet rich in vitamins C and E, zinc, lutein, and omega-3 fatty acids can help ward off age-related vision problems like macular degeneration and cataract formation. Foods high in these nutrients include leafy green vegetables, oily fish such as salmon and tuna, and nuts and seeds. For hearing, protecting your ears from excessive noise is critical. Noise-induced hearing loss is cumulative and irreversible but entirely preventable with the use of ear protection like earplugs in loud environments and keeping the volume down on personal audio devices.

In addition to lifestyle and dietary adjustments, various assistive devices and technologies can significantly improve the quality of life for those with vision and hearing impairments. For those experiencing vision loss, corrective lenses are often the first step, including glasses and contact lenses prescribed to correct refractive errors and improve focus. As conditions like cataracts progress, stronger interventions such as surgery might become necessary. Hearing aids are a common and effective tool for hearing loss. Modern hearing aids are highly customizable and can be adjusted to the specific frequencies each individual struggles to hear. Additionally, technologies such as text-to-speech tools and enhanced audio applications on smartphones can assist in daily tasks, ensuring that communication remains clear and accessible.

Regular check-ups with healthcare professionals specializing in eye and ear care are essential to catching and managing these problems early. For eyesight, visiting an optometrist or ophthalmologist for comprehensive eye exams is recommended. These check-ups should occur at least once every two years, though more frequent exams may be necessary as you age or if you have risk factors for eye diseases. For hearing, regular screenings can help detect early loss and prompt timely intervention. An audiologist can perform these tests and offer advice and treatment, including fitting for hearing aids if necessary. Establishing a routine for these screenings can ensure that you stay ahead of any significant changes that might affect your ability to engage with the world around you fully.

By understanding the typical patterns of sensory decline and taking proactive steps to protect your eyesight and hearing, you can maintain a higher quality of life and continue enjoying your daily activities with minimal disruption. Remember, early intervention is key to managing these changes effectively, allowing you to adapt smoothly and continue living life to the fullest.

8.5 Dental Health: Keeping Your Smile Bright as You Age

If you want to keep teeth white, don't smoke, don't drink dark sodas, and NO COFFEE. Yeah No...I'm just joking.

Maintaining a bright, healthy smile is more than just a boost to your confidence; it's an integral part of your overall health, especially as you age. As we navigate through the years, our dental health faces numerous challenges that can significantly impact our quality of life. Common dental issues among older adults include gum disease, tooth decay, and tooth loss—each stemming from a variety of causes and requiring specific attention to manage effectively.

Gum disease, often starting as the mild inflammation of gums known as gingivitis, can progress to more severe periodontitis if left untreated. This progression is typically facilitated by the buildup of plaque, a sticky film of bacteria formed on the teeth and gums that can harden into tartar if not removed regularly. Symptoms like swollen, red, and bleeding gums are early warning signs. If ignored, this condition can lead to the destruction of gum tissue and even bone around the teeth, eventually causing them to become loose or fall out. Tooth decay, another prevalent issue, results from the enamel being eroded by acids produced when bacteria in the mouth break down sugar. The decay can lead to cavities and infections and can contribute to tooth loss if not addressed promptly.

The importance of a rigorous daily dental care routine cannot be overstated in preventing these conditions. Brushing at least twice a day with fluoride toothpaste helps remove plaque and prevent decay, while flossing removes food particles and plaque from between the teeth and under the gum line, areas often missed by brushing alone. Using an antiseptic mouthwash can help reduce bacteria that cause plaque and gum disease. These practices are foundational not just for maintaining dental health but for preventing the exacerbation of existing issues.

Regular professional dental care is equally crucial. Regular check-ups and cleanings allow dental professionals to monitor your oral health, manage any early signs of gum disease or decay, and remove tartar build-up that cannot be addressed by brushing and flossing alone. These visits are critical as they also provide the opportunity for your dentist to conduct oral cancer screenings and offer advice or treatment options tailored to your specific needs, ensuring that minor issues don't turn into major problems.

As dental needs evolve with age, some individuals may require more advanced treatments. Dentures, for instance, are a common solution for significant tooth loss, helping to restore the appearance and functionality of your smile. While traditional dentures are removable, newer options like implant-supported dentures provide greater stability. Dental implants, another advanced treatment, involve the placement of a titanium post into the jawbone, which serves as a permanent base for a replacement tooth. Unlike dentures, implants do not require removal and can feel more like natural teeth.

Crowns, typically used to restore the shape, size, and strength of a tooth, can cover a damaged or decayed tooth or an implant. Each of these treatments has its benefits and considerations, such as cost, procedure invasiveness, and care requirements, which should be discussed with your dental care provider to determine the best option for your health and lifestyle needs.

Embracing a comprehensive approach to dental care, combining daily hygiene practices with regular professional check-ups and considering advanced treatment options when necessary, can significantly impact your dental health and general well-being. This proactive stance not only helps maintain your dental functionality and aesthetic appeal but also contributes to a healthier, more enjoyable lifestyle as you age.

In conclusion, Chapter 8 has provided extensive insights into managing and overcoming age-related challenges, from hormonal changes and chronic conditions to sensory impairments and dental health. Each section highlights the importance of proactive management and tailored strategies to maintain health and vitality. As we move into the next chapter, we will explore integrative approaches to aging, introducing alternative therapies and holistic practices that can complement traditional medical treatments, offering you a comprehensive toolkit for thriving in your later years.

Chapter 9: What Actually Helps (And What You Can't Afford Anyway)

The original version of this chapter opened with: "Imagine a world where age does not dictate capability or vitality."

I can't imagine that world because it's not my reality. Age absolutely dictates my capability. So does cumulative injury. So does limited financial resources.

But here's what I CAN tell you: I've tried some "integrative approaches" to managing pain and aging. Some helped. Some didn't—some I couldn't afford to try in the first place.

This chapter isn't about the promise of "rejuvenation of spirit and renewal of purpose" through ancient wisdom. It's about what actually works when you're dealing with chronic pain and a broken body, what you can actually afford when your finances are already strained, and what's just expensive wishful thinking.

Let me be clear upfront: I'm a believer in acupuncture. I've experienced real relief from it. I've also tried aromatherapy and massage therapy with mixed results.

But "integrative approaches" as a comprehensive aging strategy? That requires money, access, and a body that responds to treatment. I have limited amounts of all three.

9.1 Acupuncture: The One Thing That Actually Worked

Understanding What Acupuncture Is (And Isn't)

The original chapter explained acupuncture as traditional Chinese medicine involving qi (life force) flowing through meridians, with needles inserted to restore balance and stimulate natural healing.

I don't know if I believe in qi or meridians. I'm not sure the mechanism matters.

What I know is this: acupuncture provided more pain relief than most of the pharmaceutical options I tried, with fewer side effects and better results for my specific injuries.

I'm a believer of some ancient philosophies, but because it worked when other things didn't.

Here's my experience:

I went to acupuncture initially for chronic shoulder pain that wasn't responding well to conventional pain management. I was skeptical. I'd tried physical therapy, medications, injections, and chiropractic—all with limited success.

The first acupuncture session was strange. Lying there with needles in various points, some near the pain site, some nowhere near it. Waiting for something to happen.

And then... the pain reduced. Not eliminated, but noticeably reduced. The muscle tension that had been constant for months eased.

It didn't fix the underlying damage. The shoulder was still destroyed. But it made the pain more manageable for days or sometimes weeks after a session.

Benefits I Actually Experienced

The original chapter listed benefits: pain relief, improved sleep, better digestion, enhanced circulation, boosted immune system, and improved mood.

My experience:

Pain relief: YES. This was real and significant. The reduction in chronic pain after acupuncture sessions was better than most pharmaceutical options and lasted longer than I expected.

Improved sleep: Indirectly, yes. When pain is reduced, sleep improves. I don't know if acupuncture directly affects sleep or if it's just that less pain = better sleep. Either way, I slept better after sessions.

Better digestion: Didn't notice any change.

Enhanced circulation: No idea. Not something I could measure.

Boosted immune system: Can't say. I still got sick at normal rates.

Improved mood: Absolutely. When you're in less pain, your mood improves. When you sleep better, your mood improves. Whether acupuncture directly affects mood or it's all secondary to pain relief, I don't know. But yes, my mood was better when I was getting regular acupuncture.

The effect was cumulative. One session helped. Regular sessions (when I could afford them) helped more.

Why I'm Not Still Getting Acupuncture

If acupuncture worked so well, why am I not still getting it regularly?

Cost.

Acupuncture sessions aren't cheap. Depending on your location and practitioner, you're looking at $75-150 per session. Insurance coverage varies—some plans cover it partially, some don't cover it at all.

When I was getting acupuncture regularly, I was going once or twice a month. That's $150-300/month, much of which insurance didn't cover.

When you're already paying substantial out-of-pocket costs for injury-related medical care, acupuncture becomes a luxury you can't sustain long-term.

I stopped not because it didn't work, but because I couldn't afford to continue.

This is the brutal reality of "integrative approaches": they often require ongoing expenses that isn't covered by insurance. Even when they work, even when they're more effective than conventional treatments, you can't continue them if you can't pay for them.

Finding a Qualified Practitioner

The original chapter emphasized finding a certified, licensed acupuncturist who adheres to hygiene protocols.

This is important. Acupuncture involves needles. You want someone who knows what they're doing and maintains proper sterilization.

I found my acupuncturist through referrals from other people dealing with chronic pain. Looked for someone licensed in my state, checked credentials, and verified they had experience with injury-related pain.

The consultation before the first treatment was thorough—medical history, current conditions, medications, and specific pain issues. A good acupuncturist will take time to understand your situation before starting treatment.

If you're considering acupuncture:
- Verify state licensure
- Ask about their experience with your specific condition
- Discuss costs and insurance coverage upfront
- Don't be afraid to try a different practitioner if the first one doesn't work for you

Integration with Conventional Treatment

The original chapter talked about acupuncture complementing conventional medical therapies, reducing the need for pharmaceuticals.

In my experience: yes, this is accurate.

When I was getting regular acupuncture, I needed less pain medication. Not zero medication—the underlying damage still existed—but less frequent use and lower doses.

This is where acupuncture excels: not as a replacement for necessary medical treatment, but as a complement that can reduce reliance on medications that have side effects and dependency risks.

I told all my doctors I was doing acupuncture. Most were supportive or at least neutral. One orthopedist was skeptical but acknowledged that if it helped with pain management, that was valuable regardless of the mechanism.

The key is communication. Your conventional medical providers need to know about all treatments you're using, including alternative therapies.

What Acupuncture Can't Do

Acupuncture reduced my pain. It improved my quality of life during the period I could afford it.

What it didn't do:
- Repair damaged tissue
- Restore lost range of motion
- Reverse cumulative injury
- Eliminate the need for surgery when the damage is severe enough
- Provide permanent relief (effects were temporary, requiring ongoing sessions)

Acupuncture is for pain management and symptom relief. It's not healing in the sense of reversing damage.

For someone with cumulative injury, this distinction matters. Acupuncture can make your life more livable. It can't make your body less broken.

My Recommendation (With Caveats)

If you're dealing with chronic pain from injury and you can afford it: try acupuncture.

Find a licensed practitioner, commit to at least 3-5 sessions to see if it helps (one session often isn't enough to gauge effectiveness), and be honest with your conventional medical providers about what you're doing.

If it helps, factor the cost into your healthcare budget if you can. If you can't sustain it financially, at least you'll know it's an option for flare-ups or particularly difficult periods.

But understand: like everything else with cumulative injury, acupuncture is management, not a cure. It's a tool, not a solution.

And it's a tool that costs money you might not have.

9.2 Herbal Remedies: What I Haven't Tried (And Why)

The Original Claims
The original chapter discussed herbal medicine using plants and extracts to promote healing, listing specific herbs:
- Ginkgo biloba for cognitive function
- Turmeric for inflammation
- Ginseng for energy

All presented as evidence-based approaches to managing age-related conditions.

My Experience: Extremely Limited

I haven't explored herbal remedies extensively for a few reasons:

1. Cost: Quality herbal supplements aren't cheap, and insurance doesn't cover them. When you're already paying for prescription medications and other medical care, adding herbal supplements is another expense.

2. Uncertainty about efficacy: Unlike acupuncture where I experienced clear, immediate results, herbal remedies have always seemed more nebulous. Will this supplement actually help, or am I just spending money on an expensive placebo?

3. Drug interactions: I'm on multiple medications for pain management and other conditions. Adding herbal supplements means potential drug interactions that my doctors would need to

review. This requires appointments, discussions, and monitoring—more medical complexity.

4. Regulatory uncertainty: Herbal supplements aren't regulated like pharmaceuticals. Quality varies between brands. Potency varies. Contamination is possible. This makes it hard to know what you're actually getting.

What I Have Tried

Turmeric: I've used turmeric in cooking and tried turmeric supplements briefly. Did it reduce inflammation? I honestly couldn't tell. My inflammation levels are so high from cumulative injury that any reduction from turmeric was imperceptible.

I still use turmeric in cooking because it tastes good and there's no downside. But as a therapeutic intervention for serious inflammation? I saw no measurable benefit.

Generic multivitamins and supplements: I take vitamin D (because testing showed deficiency), calcium (for bone health), and a general multivitamin. These are preventive and relatively cheap.

Have they made a difference? Unknown. They might prevent things from getting worse. They haven't made things better.

What I Haven't Tried (And Probably Won't)

Ginkgo biloba for cognitive function: My cognitive issues (when they occur) are primarily from pain-disrupted sleep and chronic stress, not age-related decline. Addressing the root causes (pain management, stress reduction) seems more logical than adding a supplement.

Ginseng for energy: I'm tired because I'm dealing with chronic pain, limited sleep, and the general exhaustion of managing multiple health conditions. Ginseng won't fix those underlying causes.

Various other herbal remedies for specific conditions: Maybe some would help. But the cost-benefit analysis doesn't work when I'm already stretched thin financially.

The Drug Interaction Problem

The original chapter warned that herbs can interact with prescription medications—ginkgo can thin blood, turmeric can exacerbate anticoagulant effects.

This is a real concern. When you're on multiple medications (as many people with cumulative injury are), adding herbs means:
- Researching interactions
- Consulting with doctors (more appointments)
- Monitoring for side effects
- Potentially adjusting medication doses

This complexity is manageable if you have time, energy, and medical support. When you're already overwhelmed managing existing treatments, adding herbal remedies is just more complexity.

My Position on Herbal Remedies

I'm not against herbal medicine. I think there's value in plant-based approaches to health.

But I'm also realistic about:
- The cost of quality supplements
- The uncertainty about efficacy for severe conditions
- The complexity of integrating them with conventional treatments
- The lack of insurance coverage

For someone with limited resources dealing with serious cumulative injury, herbal remedies fall into the category of "might be helpful but can't prioritize right now."

If I had unlimited resources, I'd probably explore herbal medicine more thoroughly under professional guidance.

I don't have unlimited resources.

So herbal remedies remain in the "maybe someday" category while I focus on the treatments I know help (like acupuncture, when I can afford it) and the conventional medical care that's necessary for managing severe conditions.

If You Want to Try Herbal Remedies

If you're interested in herbal medicine and have the resources:
- Consult with a qualified herbalist or naturopathic doctor
- Research interactions with any medications you're taking
- Start with one herb at a time to gauge effects
- Buy from reputable sources (quality matters)
- Give it enough time to work (some herbs take weeks to show effects)
- Be honest with your conventional medical providers about what you're taking

Just understand: herbal remedies are supplemental. They're not replacements for necessary medical care. And they cost money that might be better spent on treatments with more established efficacy for your specific conditions.

9.3 Aromatherapy: Pleasant But Not Life-Changing

What Aromatherapy Is Supposed to Do

The original chapter described aromatherapy as using essential oils to enhance physical and emotional health, creating a sanctuary of calming fragrances.

Specific oils mentioned:
- Lavender for stress relief and sleep

- Peppermint for energy and alertness
- Eucalyptus for respiratory health

All are positioned as therapeutic interventions with real health benefits.

My Experience: Nice, But...

I've tried aromatherapy. I have a diffuser. I've used lavender oil for relaxation, peppermint for headaches, and eucalyptus when I had respiratory issues.

Did it help? Sort of. A little. Maybe.

Here's the honest assessment:

Lavender for sleep and stress: Lavender scent is pleasant. It creates a calming environment. Did it actually improve my sleep or reduce my stress in a measurable way?

I don't think so.

My sleep problems stem from chronic pain that wakes me up and keeps me awake. Lavender scent doesn't address pain. It makes the room smell good, which is... nice. But it's not a therapeutic intervention that solves the underlying problem.

My stress stems from managing chronic health conditions, financial strain, and limited physical capacity. Lavender scent doesn't reduce any of those stressors. It provides a momentary pleasant sensory experience. That's not nothing, but it's not treatment.

Peppermint for energy: Peppermint scent is invigorating. It smells fresh and sharp.

Did it actually increase my energy or alertness? No. I'm tired because of chronic pain, poor sleep, and the physical exhaustion of living in a body that doesn't work right. Peppermint scent doesn't fix any of that.

It's a pleasant smell. That's the extent of its effect.

Eucalyptus for respiratory health: When I've had congestion or respiratory issues, eucalyptus oil in a diffuser or in a hot shower did seem to help clear my airways temporarily.

This is probably the most concrete benefit I experienced from aromatherapy—actual physical relief from congestion, even if temporary.

The Overall Assessmen Aromatherapy is pleasant. It's not therapeutic in any meaningful way for the serious health issues I'm dealing with.

The diffuser costs maybe $30. The oils are relatively inexpensive. So it's not a significant financial burden.

But it's also not providing significant health benefits beyond "this smells nice and might help with minor symptoms like congestion."

When Your Problems Are Serious, Aromatherapy Is Supplemental at Best

The original chapter positioned aromatherapy as part of a holistic approach to aging, creating calming environments and addressing stress.

For someone dealing with normal age-related stress and minor sleep issues, maybe aromatherapy helps noticeably.

For someone dealing with chronic pain, severe sleep disruption from physical limitations, and the stress of managing multiple severe health conditions?

Aromatherapy is background noise. It's a nice smell in a room full of problems that smell can't solve.

I'm not saying it's worthless. Pleasant sensory experiences have value. A calming environment has value.

But let's not pretend that lavender oil in a diffuser is a meaningful intervention for serious health issues.

If You Want to Try Aromatherapy

The barrier to entry is low. A basic diffuser and a few oils will cost less than $50.

If you enjoy pleasant scents and find them relaxing, go for it. There's no real downside (aside from the cost).

Just don't expect it to solve serious health problems. It won't reduce chronic pain. It won't fix sleep disorders caused by physical issues. It won't address the root causes of stress related to weightyhealth conditions.

It will make your room smell nice. Sometimes that's enough.

9.4 Massage Therapy: Helps When You Can Get It, Unaffordable to Maintain

The Benefits Are Real
The original chapter listed massage therapy benefits:
- Improved blood circulation
- Reduced muscle tension
- Enhanced flexibility
- Joint mobility
- Anxiety and stress relief
- Better sleep

In my experience: all of this is accurate. Massage therapy does provide these benefits.

When I've had a professional massage (not often, due to cost), I've experienced:

- Temporary reduction in muscle tension
- Improved range of motion for a few days after
- Pain reduction (temporary)
- Better sleep the night after a massage
- General sense of relaxation and reduced stress

Massage therapy works. The benefits are real and noticeable.

The problem isn't efficacy. The problem is access and cost.

The Cost Barrier

Professional massage therapy runs $60-120+ per session depending on location, therapist experience, and session length.

The original chapter recommended regular sessions—monthly for general well-being, weekly or biweekly for chronic pain.

Let's do the math:

- Monthly sessions: $60-120/month = $720-1,440/year
- Biweekly sessions: $120-240/month = $1,440-2,880/year
- Weekly sessions: $240-480/month = $2,880-5,760/year

Insurance rarely covers massage therapy unless it's specifically prescribed for a medical condition and provided by a licensed medical massage therapist. Even then, coverage is often limited.

When you're already paying substantial out-of-pocket costs for injury-related medical care, regular massage therapy is a luxury most people can't afford.

I've had massage therapy occasionally—maybe 3-4 times a year when I could scrape together the money or someone gave me a gift certificate.

Each time, it helped. Each time, the benefits faded within a week or two.

To maintain the benefits, I'd need regular sessions. I can't afford regular sessions.

So massage therapy falls into the same category as acupuncture: proven to help, impossible to sustain financially.

Types of Massage for Injury-Related Pain

The original chapter discussed Swedish massage (gentle, relaxing) and deep tissue massage (more intense, for chronic tension).

In my experience:

Swedish massage is pleasant but not particularly therapeutic for serious muscle tension and injury-related pain. It's relaxing, which has value, but it doesn't address deep muscle issues.

Deep tissue massage is more effective for chronic muscle tension and pain. It can be uncomfortable during the session (sometimes quite painful), but the relief afterward is more significant and longer-lasting.

For someone with cumulative injury and chronic pain, deep tissue is usually what you need. It's also usually more expensive and more physically demanding on the therapist (which is why it costs more).

Finding the Right Therapist

The original chapter emphasized finding certified therapists experienced with older adults and specific health conditions.

This is important. Not all massage therapists understand how to work with serious injury or chronic pain conditions.

When I've sought massage therapy, I've looked for:

- Licensed massage therapist (LMT) with medical massage training
- Experience with chronic pain and injury
- Willingness to communicate about pressure, pain tolerance, and specific problem areas
- Understanding of contraindications (areas to avoid due to specific injuries)

A good therapist will do an intake assessment, ask about your health conditions and injuries, and modify their approach accordingly.

A mediocre therapist will use a one-size-fits-all approach that might help a bit but won't be optimally therapeutic.

The difference matters when you're paying $80-100 for a session.

What Massage Can't Do

Massage therapy reduces muscle tension and improves circulation.
It provides temporary pain relief and relaxation.
What it doesn't do:
- Repair damaged tissue
- Reverse cumulative injury
- Provide permanent relief (benefits are temporary)
- Replace necessary medical treatment
- Fix underlying structural problems

Like acupuncture, massage is a management, not a cure.

For someone with cumulative injury, it's a tool that helps you feel better temporarily. It doesn't make you better permanently.

The Recommendation I Wish I Could Make

If I had the financial resources, I'd get biweekly deep tissue massage therapy indefinitely.

It would significantly improve my quality of life. The pain reduction, improved mobility, and better sleep from regular massage would be worth the cost if I could afford it.

I can't afford it.

So my actual recommendation is: if you can afford regular massage therapy, and if you have chronic pain or muscle tension from injury, try it. Find a good therapist. Commit to regular sessions to see cumulative benefits.

If you can't afford it regularly, occasional sessions are still worthwhile when you can manage them. Even temporary relief is valuable.

But don't feel guilty about not being able to afford a regular massage. It's expensive, it's often not covered by insurance, and it's one more cost on top of everything else you're already paying for.

It helps. I wish I could do it more. I can't.

That's the reality for most people dealing with cumulative injury and limited finances.

9.5 Naturopathy: Sounds Great, Can't Afford It

What Naturopathy Promises

The original chapter described naturopathy as holistic, treating the whole person, addressing root causes rather than just symptoms, and focusing on the body's inherent ability to heal.

It positioned naturopathic doctors (NDs) as comprehensive practitioners who consider physical, mental, emotional, and environmental factors, creating personalized treatment plans.

For common aging concerns like hormonal imbalances, digestive issues, and chronic inflammation, naturopathy supposedly offers natural, non-invasive solutions.

This all sounds wonderful.

I haven't tried it because I can't afford it.

The Cost Reality (And the Geographic Reality)

Naturopathic consultations are expensive. Initial consultations often run $200-400 and last 60-90 minutes. Follow-up appointments are $100-200.

Then there are the recommended supplements, dietary changes, herbal remedies, and other therapies—all of which cost extra money and are not covered by insurance.

Insurance coverage for naturopathic medicine is limited. Some states require insurance to cover ND services. Most don't. Many insurance plans don't cover naturopathy at all.

When you're already paying for conventional medical care, adding naturopathic care means doubling your healthcare costs.

I can't afford to double my healthcare costs.

But here's the other barrier: I live in a small town. There are no naturopathic doctors here. None.

If I wanted to see an ND, I'd have to:
- Travel to a larger city (hours away)
- Pay for the consultation ($200-400)
- Pay for travel costs (gas, possibly hotel if it's far enough)
- Take time off for travel and appointments
- Repeat this for follow-up appointments

So even if I could somehow afford the consultation fees, the geographic barrier makes regular naturopathic care completely impractical.

This is the reality for people living outside major metropolitan areas: many "integrative approaches" simply aren't available locally. The practitioners don't exist in small towns.

You can't access care that doesn't exist in your area, regardless of whether you could afford it.

So naturopathy, regardless of its potential benefits, is doubly inaccessible to me—both financially and geographically.

The Theoretical Appeal

If I could afford it, would I try naturopathy?

Maybe.

The holistic approach appeals to me. The focus on root causes rather than just symptom management aligns with how I think about health.

The emphasis on diet, lifestyle, and natural interventions rather than pharmaceutical dependency is attractive, especially given the side effects and limitations of medications I've experienced.

But I'm also skeptical about whether naturopathy could address cumulative injury that's already caused severe structural damage.

Can dietary changes and herbal supplements reverse destroyed cartilage? No.

Can they reduce inflammation and improve overall health? Possibly.

Can they replace necessary conventional medical care? Absolutely not.

The Integration Question

The original chapter emphasized integrating naturopathy with conventional medicine.

This is where I see potential value—not as a replacement for necessary medical care, but as a complement that might reduce reliance on medications or provide additional support for managing chronic conditions.

But integration requires:
- Financial resources to pay for both naturopathic and conventional care
- Time and energy to coordinate between multiple providers
- Healthcare providers who are willing to communicate and collaborate
- Cognitive bandwidth to manage additional treatment complexity

When you're already overwhelmed managing conventional medical care for cumulative injury, adding naturopathic care is an additional complexity you might not be able to handle even if you could afford it.

My Position

I'm not opposed to naturopathy. I think holistic approaches have value.

But I'm realistic about:
- The cost barrier (prohibitive for most people with limited resources)
- The geographic barrier (doesn't exist in small towns)
- The uncertainty about efficacy for severe structural damage

- The complexity of integrating yet another healthcare approach
- The fact that insurance rarely covers it

For someone with financial resources, living in or near a major city, with relatively minor health issues, naturopathy might be valuable.

For someone dealing with serious cumulative injury, limited finances, and living in a small town where these practitioners don't exist, naturopathy is aspirational, not accessible.

Even if I won the lottery tomorrow, I'd still have to travel hours to access naturopathic care. That's a barrier that money alone can't completely solve.

Chapter Conclusion: What "Integrative Approaches" Actually Means When You're Broke

The original chapter concluded by celebrating the "transformative potential of integrating traditional healing wisdom with modern medical insights."

Here's my conclusion:

Integrative approaches to aging and health management can be valuable. I've experienced real benefits from acupuncture. I've seen temporary improvements from massage. I've found minor comfort in aromatherapy.

But here's what the original chapter didn't address:

Access is limited by finances. Most integrative therapies aren't covered by insurance. The cumulative cost of regular acupuncture, massage, herbal supplements, naturopathic care, and other alternative therapies is prohibitive for most people, especially those already struggling with medical expenses from cumulative injury.

Access is limited by geography. Many integrative practitioners don't exist in small towns. If you don't live in or near a major city, you can't access care that isn't available locally. Travel adds cost and complexity that makes regular treatment impractical.

Efficacy varies. Some approaches work for some people. Others don't. You often have to try multiple things to find what helps, which means spending money on therapies that might not work.

Integration requires resources. Managing multiple treatment approaches (conventional and alternative) requires time, energy, cognitive bandwidth, and coordination between providers. When you're already overwhelmed, integration is another burden.

Nothing reverses cumulative damage. Alternative therapies can manage symptoms, reduce pain, and improve quality of life temporarily. They cannot repair structural damage from decades of injury.

My recommendations based on actual experience:

If you can afford acupuncture and have chronic pain: try it. It worked for me better than many conventional treatments.

If you can afford occasional massage: do it when you can. The temporary relief is worth it.

If aromatherapy appeals to you: the cost is low enough that it's worth trying. Just don't expect miracles.

Herbal remedies and naturopathy: potentially valuable if you can afford them and find qualified practitioners. Most people can't afford sustained treatment.

The bottom line: "Integrative approaches" sounds like a comprehensive holistic strategy for aging well. In reality, it's a luxury available primarily to people with financial resources.

For the rest of us, it's occasional acupuncture when we can scrape together the money, pleasant-smelling oils in a diffuser, and wishing we could afford the treatments that might actually help.

That's the honest truth about integrative medicine when you're dealing with cumulative injury and limited finances.

Note: Many western doctors tend to roll their eyes at the mention of 'Alternative medicine'They flippantly dismiss the medicine that has been around longer than western civilazation and many of their remedies are successful in what they claim to do. With NO SIDE EFFECTS.

I'm not going into what I think of modern medicine what I will tell you is that whether they like it or not, they need to respect your point of view and you have to consult with them.

Chapter 10: The Complicated Truth About Aging with a Broken Body

The original version of this chapter opened with: "How often do we hear the ticking of the clock, not as a steady reminder of the present but as a countdown to what many fear as an inevitable decline?"

Here's my answer: I hear the ticking of the clock as a countdown to further decline because that's the reality I'm living in. Each year brings more deterioration, more limitations, more pain.

This chapter was supposed to be about "celebrating aging" and "positive perspectives" and "embracing later years with zest and purpose."

I can't write that chapter with a straight face.

What I CAN write is an honest assessment of what aging looks like when you're already dealing with cumulative injury, what "positive perspective" means when your body is broken, and what's actually worth celebrating versus what's toxic positivity.

This isn't the inspiring chapter about aging gracefully that was originally written. It's the complicated truth about aging with dignity despite circumstances that make "grace" nearly impossible.

10.1 Age Positivity vs. Reality: Finding Balance Between Hope and Honesty

What "Age Positivity" Is Supposed to Mean

The original chapter talked about redefining aging as "a period brimming with potential" rather than a time of decline.

It cited research showing that positive outlooks on aging lead to better health outcomes, longer life, and better recovery from health setbacks.

It encouraged viewing aging as "an opportunity for continued growth."

All of this sounds wonderful for people aging with healthy bodies.

For someone aging with a body destroyed by cumulative injury? This "age positivity" rhetoric can feel like gaslighting.

The Reality Check

I'm 58. I have a reverse total shoulder replacement—hardware where my shoulder used to be. I'm looking at a second mortgage to cover debt accumulated from decades of injury-related medical expenses. I can't work outside the home. My mobility is limited. My pain is chronic.

Can I "redefine" this as "a period brimming with potential"?

I can try. But pretending my limitations don't exist isn't positive thinking—it's denial.

Here's what I've learned about actual age positivity versus toxic positivity:

Toxic positivity says: "Aging is just a mindset! Stay positive and you'll be healthy!"

Actual age positivity says: "Aging brings real challenges, and I can find meaning and purpose despite those challenges."

Toxic positivity says: "You're only as old as you feel!"

Actual age positivity says: "I feel old because my body is damaged, and that's the truth I'm working with."

Toxic positivity says: "Don't focus on limitations, focus on possibilities!"

Actual age positivity says: "I acknowledge my limitations and find possibilities within those constraints."

The difference matters.

The Research on Positive Aging (And Its Limits)

The original chapter cited studies showing that positive outlooks on aging improve health outcomes.

This research is real. Mindset does affect health. People who view aging positively tend to have better outcomes than people who view it negatively.

But here's what the research doesn't account for:

The difference between normal aging and aging with cumulative injury. The studies look at general populations, not people with severe physical damage from decades of injury.

The causation question. Do people have positive outlooks BECAUSE they're healthier? Or does the positive outlook CAUSE better health? The relationship isn't as simple as "think positively and you'll age better."

The limits of mindset. No amount of positive thinking repairs destroyed cartilage, reverses structural damage, or eliminates chronic pain. Mindset can help you cope. It can't heal your body.

I believe in the value of a positive outlook. I've experienced how attitude affects quality of life.

But I refuse to pretend that "staying positive" is a cure for serious physical damage.

What Age Positivity Actually Means When Your Body is Broken

Here's my version of age positivity:

I'm aging with a broken body. That's the truth.

Within those constraints, I can still find meaning, purpose, and occasional joy.

I acknowledge my limitations without letting them define my entire identity.

I grieve what I've lost while protecting what I still have.

I'm honest about the hard parts while remaining open to good moments.

I reject the narrative that I failed because my body is damaged. The damage happened. I'm managing it.

This isn't the cheerful "embrace aging with zest!" message of the original chapter.

But it's honest. And it's sustainable.

Toxic positivity creates shame when you can't maintain the cheerful facade. Honest positivity allows for the full range of human experience—pain and joy, grief and gratitude, struggle and occasional triumph.

The Language We Use About Aging

The original chapter discussed how language shapes perceptions of aging—avoiding terms like "silver tsunami" in favor of "age of opportunity."

I agree that language matters.

But I also think we need language that acknowledges reality.

Terms I reject:
- "Golden years" (implies wealth and ease that many don't have)
- "Aging gracefully" (implies there's a right and wrong way to age)
- "You're only as old as you feel" (dismisses real physical limitations)
- "Age is just a number" (tell that to my destroyed shoulder)

Terms that feel more honest:
- "Aging with intention" (making deliberate choices within constraints)
- "Aging with dignity" (maintaining self-respect despite challenges)
- "Later years" or "older adulthood" (neutral, descriptive)
- "Managing aging" (acknowledges it requires active work)

Language that acknowledges both challenges and possibilities feels more authentic than language that pretends everything is wonderful.

Combating Ageism While Being Honest About Limitations

The original chapter discussed combating ageism—the stereotyping and discrimination against people because of age.

Ageism is real and harmful. Older people are stereotyped as incompetent, irrelevant, or burdensome.

This needs to be challenged.

But here's the complexity: I can fight ageism while also being honest about my limitations.

Fighting ageism means: Refusing to accept that my value decreases because I'm older. Challenging assumptions that older people can't contribute or learn or matter.

Being honest about limitations means: Acknowledging that I can't do everything I used to do. Recognizing that my body has real constraints that affect what's possible.

These aren't contradictory. I can have value AND have limitations. My worth isn't determined by my physical capabilities.

The problem is when society conflates aging with worthlessness. That's ageism, and it's wrong.

But the solution isn't pretending limitations don't exist. It insists that people have value regardless of limitations.

What I Actually Celebrate About Aging

The original chapter wanted me to celebrate aging as an opportunity for growth.

Here's what I actually appreciate about being 58:

I know myself better than I did at 25 or 35 or 45. The self-knowledge that comes with decades of experience is invaluable.

I care less about other people's opinions. Age brings freedom from the need to prove myself constantly.

I have perspective on what matters. Decades of experience teach you to distinguish between real problems and temporary irritations.

I've survived things I didn't think I could survive. That builds a certain resilience and confidence.

I'm writing this book. Sharing hard-won knowledge might help someone avoid the mistakes I made. That matters.

These aren't the glossy "celebrating my best life!" celebrations of typical age-positivity rhetoric.

But they're real. And they matter.

Aging has brought losses—significant, painful losses. But it's also brought some gains. Both can be true simultaneously.

10.2 Hobbies and Passions: What's Possible Within Constraints

The Original Vision

The original chapter opened with: "Imagine a canvas, blank and vast, waiting for the vibrant colors of your experiences to bring it to life."

Then it talked about rediscovering old hobbies (guitar, painting, poetry) or exploring new ones (digital photography, writing, bird watching).

It positioned hobbies as mental stimulation, emotional satisfaction, social connection, and cognitive health.

All of this is accurate for people with the time, energy, and physical capacity to pursue hobbies.

The Reality of Limited Energy and Physical Constraints

I write. That's my hobby and my work now.

Not because I chose writing as the perfect later-life passion, but because writing is one of the few things I can still do despite physical limitations.

I can't play guitar (destroyed shoulder, limited range of motion). I can't do photography that requires traveling or physical mobility. I can't do crafts that require fine motor control or sustained physical positioning. I can't do bird watching that requires hiking or extended standing.

The hobbies available to me are constrained by what my body can physically manage.

Writing works because:
- I can do it sitting down
- I can take breaks when pain flares
- I can work on my own schedule
- It doesn't require physical mobility
- It provides mental engagement without physical demands

This isn't "rediscovering my passion for writing." This is "writing is one of the few things my broken body can still do."

That sounds cynical. But it's honest.

What Hobbies Actually Provide (And Don't Provide)

The original chapter listed the benefits of hobbies:
- Mental stimulation (keeps the mind sharp)
- Emotional satisfaction (enhances mood)
- Social connection (widens social network)
- Cognitive health (improves brain function)

In my experience with writing:

Mental stimulation: Yes. Writing this book requires research, organization, and clear thinking. It keeps my brain engaged.

Emotional satisfaction: Sometimes. Writing about difficult experiences can be draining as well as satisfying. It's not pure joy. It's complicated.

Social connection: Limited. Writing is mostly solitary. I'm not joining writing groups or attending workshops because of mobility and energy constraints.

Cognitive health: Probably. Using my brain intensively likely helps maintain cognitive function. But I can't measure this.

So hobbies do provide value. But they're not the pure source of joy and fulfillment that the original chapter suggested.

They're what's possible within severe constraints.

Finding What Works Within Your Limitations

If you're aging with cumulative injury or other physical limitations, here's my actual advice about hobbies:

Assess what you can physically do. Be honest about your constraints. Don't set yourself up for failure by choosing hobbies your body can't handle.

Consider low-physical-demand activities:
- Reading (if vision allows)
- Writing (if you can sit and type)
- Audiobooks or podcasts (if hearing allows)
- Gentle crafts that don't require sustained positioning
- Online communities related to your interests
- Bird watching from a window if you can't hike

Adjust your expectations. Your hobby doesn't have to be impressive or productive. It just has to be something you can do that provides some engagement or satisfaction.

Accept that energy is limited. You might only have capacity for 30 minutes a day. That's okay. Do what you can.

Don't compare yourself to healthy people pursuing elaborate hobbies. Their constraints are different from yours.

The Resources Question

The original chapter mentioned community centers, libraries, online classes, and YouTube tutorials.

All of these exist. Some are free or low-cost.

But accessing them requires:
- Transportation (if not online)
- Energy to participate
- Cognitive bandwidth to learn new things
- Sometimes money for materials or subscriptions

When you're dealing with chronic pain, limited mobility, and financial strain, even "free" resources require resources you might not have.

I use YouTube for information sometimes. I can't attend classes at community centers because getting there and sitting through a class exceeds my physical capacity.

Online learning is more accessible for people with physical limitations. But it still requires energy and focus that chronic pain can deplete.

Be realistic about what you can actually access and sustain.

What Actually Matters About Hobbies

The original chapter positioned hobbies as essential for a "rich and fulfilling life" in later years.

Here's what I think actually matters:

Having something that engages your mind, even minimally, is better than having nothing.

Finding small satisfactions within severe constraints is a skill worth developing.

Hobbies don't have to be impressive to be valuable.

It's okay if your hobby is just "thing I can do that isn't completely miserable."

Not having elaborate hobbies doesn't mean you're failing at aging.

The goal isn't to become a master photographer or accomplished musician in your later years.

The goal is to find whatever engagement is possible within your constraints and be okay with that being enough.

10.3 Role Models: The Complicated Truth About Who We Can Actually Emulate

The Original Narrative

The original chapter showcased "individuals who have embraced their later years with zest and purpose."

Example given: A 70-year-old retired teacher who started a second career as a community organizer.

The message: Look at these inspiring people! You can be like them! Aging is full of possibilities!

The lessons: Maintain a positive attitude, stay physically active, engage in community, and view challenges as opportunities.

This is inspiring... if you have the health and resources to emulate these role models.

The Problem with Aspirational Role Models

When you're dealing with cumulative injury, chronic pain, and severe physical limitations, role models who are "thriving in their later years" can feel more discouraging than inspiring.

I can't become a community organizer. That requires energy, mobility, and physical capacity I don't have.

I can't start a second career in most fields. My body limits what work I can do.

I can't be "vibrant and engaged" in the way these role models are portrayed.

Does that mean I'm failing at aging? Does that mean I'm not a "good" role model?

The original chapter's framing suggests that successful aging looks like continued high activity and achievement.

What about people who are just trying to survive with dignity despite severe constraints?

Where are the role models for THAT?

Who I Actually Look To

My actual role models aren't the 70-year-olds running marathons or starting businesses or traveling the world.

My role models are:

People managing chronic illness with honesty and without shame.

People find meaning despite severe physical limitations.

People speaking truthfully about the hard parts of aging instead of maintaining a cheerful facade.

People who acknowledge grief while still getting up each day.

People who have learned to measure success by survival rather than achievement.

These aren't the role models featured in "positive aging" books.

But they're the role models I need.

The Lessons I've Actually Learned

The original chapter talked about lessons from role models: positive attitude, proactive health approach, viewing challenges as opportunities.

Here are the actual lessons I've learned from people aging with serious limitations:

Survival is enough. You don't have to thrive to matter. Getting through each day with dignity is an achievement.

Honesty is more sustainable than positivity. Acknowledging hard truths allows you to address them. Toxic positivity creates shame.

Grief is part of the process. You can grieve what you've lost while still living. Both can coexist.

Adaptation is necessary. You can't do what you used to do. Finding new ways to matter requires accepting that reality.

Value isn't determined by productivity. You have worth regardless of what you can accomplish.

These lessons don't make for inspiring magazine articles. But they're what actually help when you're aging with a broken body.

Being a Role Model Within Constraints

The original chapter encouraged being a role model by "embodying admirable qualities" and "leading by example."

Here's what being a role model looks like when you're dealing with cumulative injury:

Writing this book. Sharing honest experience so younger people might avoid my mistakes.

Being truthful about challenges. Not pretending everything is fine when it isn't.

Showing that dignity is possible despite limitations. You can age with self-respect even when you can't age "gracefully."

Refusing to be ashamed. Physical limitations don't make you less valuable.

Acknowledging both pain and occasional joy. Life is complicated—especially—when you're struggling.

I'm not the inspiring 70-year-old starting a new career. I'm the 58-year-old with hardware in her shoulder, writing from home because it's the work she can still do.

That's the role model I can be. And maybe that matters more than another story about vibrant, active aging.

Engaging with Younger Generations

The original chapter talked about sharing wisdom with younger people through mentorship, intergenerational projects, and teaching skills.

Here's what I can actually offer:

Warning. This is what happens when you push through pain.

 Learn from my mistakes.

Honesty. Aging isn't all positive. Here's the complicated truth.

Perspective. I've survived things I didn't think I could survive. You might too.

Practical knowledge. Here's what actually works and what doesn't when you're managing chronic conditions.

This isn't the cheerful intergenerational bonding of the original chapter.

But it might be more valuable. Young people need to know the truth about cumulative consequences, not just inspiring stories about possibilities.

If sharing my experience prevents even one person from destroying their body the way I did, that's meaningful engagement with younger generations.

Conclusion: This Is the Part Where You Face the Truth

I can't give you your power back.

If cumulative injury took it, if decades of damage stole it, if chronic pain and limited mobility and financial devastation claimed it—I can't hand it back to you in a neat conclusion with inspiring bullet points.

That's not how this works.

What I CAN give you is this: the truth about what "no pain, no gain" actually costs, told by someone who's paid that cost for thirty years and is still paying it.

The truth is complicated. It's not inspiring. It's not empowering in the way self-help books promise empowerment.

But it's real. And real is what you need.

What This Book Was Actually About

This wasn't a book about "ageless living" or "thriving in your later years" or "embracing aging with vitality."

Those books exist. They're written by people whose bodies cooperated with their aspirations.

This was a book about consequences.

The consequence of pushing through pain in your 20s is chronic pain in your 50s.

The consequence of "just getting it done" despite injury is a body that can't get much done three decades later.

The consequence of proving you're not weak is becoming weak in ways you can't reverse.

The consequence of crash dieting for fitness tests is metabolic damage that persists for life.

The consequence of cumulative injury is cumulative cost—medical, financial, physical, and emotional.

These consequences compound. They multiply. They don't go away because you finally understand them.

I'm 58 with hardware where my shoulder used to be. I'm looking at a second mortgage to cover debt from publishing and medical expenses that trace back to injuries from my 20s and 30s. I can't work outside the home. My mobility is limited. My pain is chronic.

Understanding why this happened doesn't fix it.

But understanding might—MIGHT—prevent you from creating the same consequences in your own life.

That's the only power I can offer: knowledge before it's too late.

What I'm NOT Telling You

I'm not telling you that positive thinking heals cumulative injury.

I'm not telling you that the right supplements reverse structural damage.

I'm not telling you to "refuse to fade" when your body is forcing you to adapt.

I'm not telling you that aging is just a mindset.

I'm not telling you that you can have the same capabilities at 60 that you had at 30.

I'm not selling you inspiration. I'm offering you a warning.

The difference matters.

What I AM Telling You

If you're young—20s, 30s, early 40s—and you're pushing through pain to prove something:

Stop.

The pain is information. Your body is telling you something is wrong. Ignoring that information doesn't make you strong. It makes you injured.

The injury you're creating today will cost you for decades. Medical expenses. Lost income. Reduced mobility. Chronic pain. Financial strain. Limited options.

Every time you push through pain, you're taking out a loan against your future body. The interest rate is brutal.

If you're already dealing with cumulative injury—if you're living the consequences I've described:

You're not alone.

The 45-year-old has destroyed knees from running through injuries. The 52-year-old who can't afford the treatments that would help. The 60-year-old is managing chronic pain and limited mobility.

This book doesn't fix your situation. But it acknowledges it honestly, without the toxic positivity that makes you feel like you failed for having a broken body.

You didn't fail. The system that told you to push through pain failed you.

You're managing the aftermath as best you can. That's enough.

What "Taking Power Back" Actually Means

The original conclusion talked about "taking power back" and "refusing to become irrelevant."

Here's what taking power back actually looks like when you're dealing with cumulative injury:

Acknowledging reality without shame. Your body is damaged. That's the truth. You don't have to pretend otherwise.

Making decisions within constraints. You can't do everything you used to do. You CAN decide what's possible within your limitations.

Protecting what you still have. You can't reverse damage. You CAN prevent additional damage.

Finding meaning despite limitations. Your life has value regardless of your physical capabilities.

Refusing to accept toxic positivity. You don't have to be cheerful about chronic pain to have dignity.

Sharing truth. Warning others about consequences they can still prevent.

This isn't the dramatic "seizing power" moment of typical conclusions.

It's quieter than that. More complicated. Less inspiring but more sustainable.

It's the power of honesty in a world that demands cheerful facades.

It's the power of survival when thriving isn't an option.

It's the power of dignity despite circumstances that make grace nearly impossible.

The Two Audiences for This Book

If you're young and healthy:

This book is your warning. Don't do what I did. Don't ignore pain. Don't prove your toughness by destroying your body. Don't create consequences that will define your next thirty years.

The short-term gain (passing a fitness test, impressing someone, proving you're not weak) is not worth the long-term cost.

Protect your body now. You only get one.

If you're already living with cumulative injury:

This book is your witness. Someone sees you. Someone understands. The pain is real. The limitations are real. The financial strain is real. The grief is real.

You're not failing because you can't maintain the cheerful "aging with vitality!" narrative.

You're surviving with whatever dignity you can maintain despite circumstances that make everything harder.

That's enough. You're enough.

What Happens After This Book

I don't know what happens to you after you close this book.

Maybe you're young and you'll actually heed the warning. Maybe you'll protect your body in ways I didn't. Maybe you'll avoid the consequences I'm living with.

Maybe you're already dealing with cumulative injury and you just needed someone to acknowledge that it's hard without offering false solutions.

Maybe this book made you angry. Maybe it depressed you. Maybe it validated something you already knew but couldn't articulate.

I don't know.

What I do know:

The truth about "no pain, no gain" is that the pain doesn't go away, and the gain is temporary.

The truth about cumulative injury is that the costs compound for decades.

The truth about aging with a broken body is that it's exponentially harder than aging with a healthy one.

The truth about surviving despite severe limitations is that survival itself is an achievement, even when it doesn't feel like one.

The truth about this book is that it's not inspiring, but it's honest.

And honest is what I have to offer.

Final Words

I'm not going to end with a rousing call to action about seizing your power and refusing to fade.

That's not my reality. It might not be yours either.

Instead, I'll end with this:

If you're young: The choices you make about your body today will echo for decades. Choose carefully. Pain is information, not weakness. Listen to it.

If you're already broken: You have value regardless of what your body can do. Survival with dignity is enough. You're enough.

If you're somewhere in between: You still have time to protect what you have. You can't reverse existing damage, but you can prevent additional damage.

That's the power I can offer: knowledge, honesty, and acknowledgment.

It's not the power to turn back time or heal cumulative injury or make aging easy.

But it's real.

And real is what you need.

Thank you for reading.

Take care of your body. It's the only one you get.

And if your body is already broken—take care of yourself anyway. You still matter.

That's the truth this book has been building toward.

Not inspiration. Not empowerment. Not ageless vitality.

Just truth.

Truth about consequences.

Truth about costs.

Truth about survival.

Truth about dignity despite damage.

That's what I have to offer.

I hope it's enough.

References

- *Nutrition Guide: What to eat and what not in your 20s, 30s, 40s and beyond* https://m.economictimes.com/news/how-to/nutrition-guide-what-to-eat-and-what-not-in-your-20s-30s-40s-and-beyond/articleshow/103403916.cms

- *Growing Stronger - Strength Training for Older Adults - CDC* https://www.cdc.gov/physicalactivity/downloads/growing_stronger.pdf

- *Stress Management: Techniques & Strategies to Deal with ...* https://www.helpguide.org/articles/stress/stress-management.htm

- *Consistent sleep slows down aging at a cellular level* https://www.earth.com/news/consistent-sleep-slows-down-aging-at-a-cellular-level/

- *How Mindfulness Affects the Brain | Made of Millions Foundation* https://www.madeofmillions.com/articles/how-mindfulness-affects-the-brain

- *Midlife Crisis: Signs, Causes, and Coping Tips* https://www.helpguide.org/articles/aging-issues/midlife-crisis.htm

- *Positive Psychology: Harnessing the power of happiness, mindfulness, and inner strength* https://www.health.harvard.edu/mind-and-mood/positive-psychology-harnessing-the-power-of-happiness-mindfulness-and-inner-strength

- *How to Handle Life's Transitions Through Emotional Intelligence* https://www.isei.com/blog/how-to-handle-life-s-transitions-through-emotional-intelligence

- *Functional Exercises for Seniors: Improve Balance and ...* https://www.silversneakers.com/blog/functional-fitness-the-silversneakers-guide/

- *Pilates for Beginners: A Complete Guide* https://www.menshealth.com/uk/fitness/lifestyle/a36590832/pilates/

- *3 Kinds of Exercise That Boost Heart Health* https://www.hopkinsmedicine.org/health/wellness-and-prevention/3-kinds-of-exercise-that-boost-heart-health

- *Fall Prevention: Balance and Strength Exercises for Older ...* https://www.hopkinsmedicine.org/health/wellness-and-prevention/fall-prevention-exercises

- *Anti-Inflammatory Diets - StatPearls* https://www.ncbi.nlm.nih.gov/books/NBK597377/

- *Free radicals, antioxidants and functional foods: Impact on ...* https://www.ncbi.nlm.nih.gov/pmc/articles/PMC3249911/

- *Top meal planning resources for senior caregivers - Seasons* https://www.seasons.com/top-meal-planning-resources-for-senior-caregivers/2623371/

- *Vitamins Your Body Will Need as You Age* https://www.bannerhealth.com/healthcareblog/advise-me/vitamins-what-you-should-take-at-every-age

- *Social engagement and health outcomes among older ...* https://www.ncbi.nlm.nih.gov/pmc/articles/PMC5547666/

- *9 Of The Best Volunteering Opportunities For Seniors* https://www.liveatwhitestone.org/news/best-volunteering-opportunities-for-seniors/

- *Digital Literacy for Senior Citizens: Building ICT ...* https://ctu.ieee.org/digital-literacy-for-senior-citizens-building-ict-competencies/

- *Intergenerational Activity* https://generationsworkingtogether.org/downloads/5bebf57b90d25-Intergenerational-Activity-Guide-2018-St-Monica-Trust.pdf

- *Approach to preventive care in the elderly - PMC* https://www.ncbi.nlm.nih.gov/pmc/articles/PMC5023341/

- *Your guide to preventative health screenings you should get in your 40s* https://www.cbsnews.com/news/preventative-health-tests-screenings-age-40s/

- *Recommendations for Screening Older Patients for Depression* https://www.mentalhealthandaging.com/recommendations-for-screening-older-patients-for-depression/

- *The Future of Health Screening: Innovations and Technology* https://hmedicalcentre.com/the-future-of-health-screening-innovations-and-technology/#:~:text=These%20technologies%20enable%20patients%20to,manage%20their%20health%20more%20effectively.

- *How to plan for rising health care costs* https://www.fidelity.com/viewpoints/personal-finance/plan-for-rising-health-care-costs

- *7 High-Return, Low-Risk Investments for Retirees*
  https://money.usnews.com/investing/articles/high-return-low-risk-investments-for-retirees

- *What's Medicare Supplement Insurance (Medigap)?*
  https://www.medicare.gov/health-drug-plans/medigap

- *Estate Planning: 16 Things to Do Before You Die*
  https://www.investopedia.com/articles/retirement/10/estate-planning-checklist.asp

- *Health-Monitoring Devices and Apps for Seniors*
  https://bethesdahealth.org/blog/2024/01/09/health-monitoring-devices-and-apps-for-seniors/

- *The Best Smart Home Devices to Help Aging in Place*
  https://www.nytimes.com/wirecutter/reviews/smart-home-for-seniors/

- *Top 5 Online Learning Sites for Older Adults*
  https://growingbolder.com/stories/top-5-online-learning-sites-for-older-adults/

- *Telemedicine in the primary care of older adults*
  https://www.ncbi.nlm.nih.gov/pmc/articles/PMC10357882/

- *Osteoarthritis | National Institute on Aging*
  https://www.nia.nih.gov/health/osteoarthritis/osteoarthritis

- *Aging and Sleep: How Does Growing Old Affect Sleep?*
  https://www.sleepfoundation.org/aging-and-sleep

- *Assistive Devices for People with Hearing, Voice, Speech ...*
  https://www.nidcd.nih.gov/health/assistive-devices-people-hearing-voice-speech-or-language-disorders

- *Healthy gut, healthier aging - Harvard Health*
  https://www.health.harvard.edu/staying-healthy/healthy-gut-healthier-aging

- *Hobby engagement and mental well-being among people* ...
  https://www.ncbi.nlm.nih.gov/pmc/articles/PMC10504079/#:~:text=A%20meta%2Danalysis%20of%20longitudinal,expectancy%20and%20national%20happiness%20levels.

- *How To Start A Mentorship Program: A Complete Step-By-Step Guide-* ...
  https://www.forbes.com/sites/forbesbusinesscouncil/2022/06/02/how-to-start-a-mentorship-program-a-complete-step-by-step-guide/

- *Volunteering and Health for Aging Populations*
  https://www.prb.org/resources/volunteering-and-health-for-aging-populations/

- *Successful Seniors: 10 Stories of Purpose Discovered* ...
  https://www.friendship.us/insights/successful-seniors